Global Warming

GLOBAL WARMING

Jean F. Blashfield and Wallace B. Black

Education Consultant
Helen J. Challand, Ph.D.
Professor of Science Education, National-Louis University

Global Warming Consultant
Stephen P. Leatherman, Ph.D.
Director, Laboratory for Coastal Research
University of Maryland

CHILDRENS PRESS®
CHICAGO

A production of B&B Publishing, Inc.

Project Editor: Jean Blashfield Black
Designer: Elizabeth B. Graf
Computer Makeup: Dori Bechtel

Photo Researcher: Terri Willis
Cover Design: Margrit Fiddle
Artist: Valerie A. Valusek

Printed on Evergreen Gloss
50% recycled preconsumer waste
Binder's board made from 100% recycled material

Cover photograph - © Imtek Imagineering/Masterfile

Library of Congress Cataloging-in-Publication Data

Blashfield, Jean F.
    Global warming / by Jean F. Blashfield and Wallace B. Black.
        p. cm. -- (Saving planet earth)
    Includes index.
    Summary: Describes the gradual warming of our planet, its causes
and effects, and ways in which we can all help.
    ISBN 0-516-05501-1
    1. Global warming--Juvenile literature. [1. Global warming.]
I. Black, Wallace B.   II. Title   III. Series.
QC981.8.G56B55 1991
363.73'87--dc20   91-7119
                                            CIP
                                          AC

TABLE OF CONTENTS

Chapter 1

"The Year the Earth Spoke Back"

The clock's alarm shrills in your ear. You leap from your cot to your feet in an instant. Ignoring the smoky smell and dirt on your clothing, you pull on your boots and jacket. You feel as if you've made the same moves a thousand times. You've been fighting the forest fire in the foothills of eastern Pennsylvania for weeks.

It's the year 2044, and forest fires are a regular part of life. You often think that people might just as well let them burn, but all too often the flames lick at the edges of populated areas. No, they must be fought, and that's your job.

Quickly grabbing a glass of juice, you head back to the fireline, knowing you won't rest again for many hours. The air is thick with an almost touchable heat that you know isn't all from the fire. Even when the fire is out, there will be no relief from the heat until autumn. The weather forecasters are predicting another month of temperatures in the nineties or even higher before there is any chance of a slight cooling.

As you look at the fire-blackened trees around you, you think how much more devastating a forest fire would have been a century ago. Then the forests of the East Coast were healthy and green. But now most of the beech, maple, oak, and other trees of the area have been weakened by the high temperatures and frequent droughts that are a normal part of life today. Some species were able to survive in newly warm Canadian lands, but others couldn't adjust to the rocky soil of eastern Canada, and they died out. What you're fighting to save is the last remnants of those forests.

Thinking of Canada, you decide that you'll go there for your vacation this year—if you can get a train ticket, everyone seems to be going to Canada. You wish you could go to your grandparents' farm in Iowa, at least to the Iowa your parents told you about—a green place that was crisply cold in winter and pleasantly sunny in summer, with fields of corn as far as the eye could see.

But that was forty or fifty years ago. The global warming that people of the late twentieth century failed to heed has changed all that. Your grandparents, whose family had owned the farm for generations, went bankrupt last year after the fifth year of drought in a row. There wasn't much plantable land left anyway, it had been covered with sand blowing up from Texas.

Sometimes you find it hard to believe that the Iowa area used to be called the "Breadbasket of the World," and that the United States used to supply food to the rest of the world. Now the United States has to import grain from Canada, which was able to open up lots of land to farming as the Earth got warmer. Unfortunately, the Canadians cut down a lot of forest to make farmland, which, of course, contributed to the warming.

You stop by a water pipe to refill your canteen. You're glad you can get good-tasting fresh water here in Pennsylvania. You have friends who live in Florida, or what's left of Florida. All the water supplies there seem to have been invaded by the sea.

Much of the southern tip of Florida is gone—it disappeared into the ocean as the sea level rose. You've seen photos of beautiful homes built along rivers and canals in southern Florida. The houses are still there, but they've been flooded with seawater or walled up like medieval castles.

The Mississippi Delta is gone, too, as is Egypt's Nile D̶ You've seen news programs about refugees from the

The Florida panther, already seriously endangered by highways and other human development, will lose what remains of its habitat in the Everglades if global warming causes the sea to rise.

Nile and from Bangladesh trying to find new homes. You feel sorry for all those people, but your mind balks at trying to deal with the idea of 50 or 60 million refugees. The number's too big.

If you get a break later today, you might try to find a car going into the city. You can't drive alone—you'll be arrested. Except in emergencies, there has to be at least two people in a car, even if it is fueled by hydrogen, which doesn't put more carbon dioxide into the atmosphere the way gasoline used to do.

Anyway, it's not much fun going into the city at night, not since they decided to save on fuel by turning off the lights. Sometimes you think such measures are foolish—it's too late to do anything about the gases in the atmosphere that have warmed up the planet so much. Well, we have to try, you think. It's too bad people back in the twentieth century didn't try when they had the chance. Life might be a lot more pleasant today.

Well, it's time to get back to fighting this fire that should never have happened. It's someone else's turn to take a break.

The Summer of 1988

Major forest fires and the dryness that causes them are not just a thing of the future. There were more forest fires in 1987 and 1988 in North America than ever before recorded. Almost 10 million acres (over 4 million hectares) of wildlife habitat were destroyed. A million of those acres were in Yellowstone, the oldest national park in the world.

In the summer of 1988, 35 states experienced extreme drought. Not since 1934, when the Dust Bowl was at its worst, had the central United States been so dry.

Also in 1988, in early September, Hurricane Gilbert began to form. The abnormal heat of the air had warmed the

September of 1988 gave birth to the largest Caribbean hurricane ever recorded. The winds spawned by Hurricane Gilbert were strong enough to lift this ship onto the land, where it damaged a hotel at Cancun, Mexico.

water of the Caribbean beyond its normal level. The whirling mass of air drew heat from the ocean until it became the largest hurricane ever recorded in the Western Hemisphere. Its 500-mile (800-kilometer)-wide mass traveled 2,500 miles (4,000 kilometers) along the Mexican and American borders before it broke up in the North Atlantic.

It really seemed as if this series of disasters must have a special reason behind it. President George Bush, in discussing the chain of environmental disasters, called 1988 "the year the Earth spoke back."

Then 1989 reverted back to normal temperatures. That reversion made many people suggest that the scientists had been wrong, that it was just a climatic fluke that the 1980s had the five hottest years on record. But changes in climate do not necessarily happen in a nice smooth pattern. 1990 returned to being warmer than usual.

From 1880, when weather records started to be kept, until 1950, the average global temperature rose 1 degree Fahrenheit (0.5 degrees Celsius). That means that if you take all the temperatures from all over the world and average

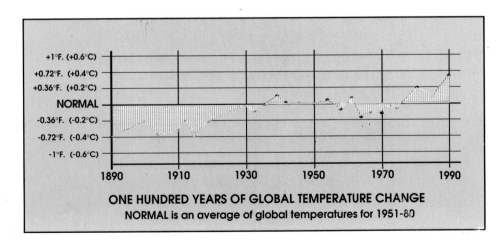

ONE HUNDRED YEARS OF GLOBAL TEMPERATURE CHANGE
NORMAL is an average of global temperatures for 1951-80

Average global temperatures have risen for more than one hundred years. This graph goes upward and downward from normal—the average of temperatures for the years 1951 to 1980. It reveals that there was a cool period in the 1960s, but the trend continued to rise.

them out, you would find an increase of 1 degree Fahrenheit over 70 years. Over the next 30 years, 1950-1980, the temperature rose another degree. Then, in the late 1980s, it rose almost as much in a much shorter time.

On a June day in 1989, when the temperature was 99 degrees F. (38 degrees C) in Washington, D.C., James Hansen of the National Aeronautics and Space Administration appeared before a congressional hearing on climate change. He said, "It is time to stop waffling so much. The evidence is pretty strong that the greenhouse effect is here."

Summers of the Future

Such temperature increases could be just normal variations in climate that will even themselves out over the coming century. However, they could also mean the start of big trouble for our planet.

Life on Earth depends on the greenhouse effect—the trapping of heat from sunlight within the atmosphere by certain gases. Without the greenhouse effect, Earth would be much too cold for life to have developed. But human activities have been adding more heat-trapping gases to the atmosphere than is normal. The temperature of the entire planet appears to be rising.

Most climate scientists agree that global warming is taking place. They think that Earth's temperature will rise another 1.8 to 3.5 degrees F. (1 to 2 degrees C) by 2030, and 3 to 8 degrees F. (1.5 to 4.5 degrees C) by 2050, unless we do something to stop it. After the last Ice Age, it took 18,000 years for the temperature of the planet to rise 9 degrees F. (5 degrees C), and it may increase by at least half that amount in just the next *sixty* years.

The smoke and heat of a forest fire may last only a few days, but the heat and drought of a world made too warm by human carelessness could last forever.

This is a book of "probably" and "maybe." No one knows for sure that these temperature changes and all the resulting predicted effects are going to happen during the next fifty years. No one knows for sure whether the effects in any particular area will be good or bad. But we have to act as if we were certain that they were going to happen. If we don't, it will be too late to stop them, once our "probably" has turned to "it is."

Albert Einstein said, "Civilization is a race between education and disaster." We have to quickly educate ourselves and the rest of the world to the need for change, or we will end in disaster. We must start now to make changes in the way we live in order to prevent the worst from happening. We humans made the problem, and we have the ability to unmake it—if we have the will.

Chapter 2

The Greenhouse Effect

As far as we know, Earth is the only planet in our solar system that has the right conditions for life. Also, as far as we know, human beings are the only form of life on Earth that has the ability to affect, in any major way, those very conditions that let us live. We've taken the resources that the planet gave us and turned them against ourselves.

Among the conditions that allowed life as we know it to develop are sunlight and an atmosphere of the right gases. The air we breathe is a mixture of gases. It consists of 78 percent nitrogen (N_2) and 21 percent oxygen (O_2). Gases called *trace* gases make up the remaining 1 percent. They include water vapor, carbon dioxide, methane, and ozone, a variety of oxygen with three atoms to a molecule instead of two.

The interaction of sunlight and those trace gases is vital to the future of our planet.

Trapping Sunlight. Sunlight is a mixture of many wavelengths of energy, some of them visible. About 30 percent of the energy in sunlight is reflected back into space by Earth's oceans and clouds. The remaining 70 percent is absorbed by the planet, which is warmed by it. Anything that's warm gives off, or emits, heat. The heat radiates from Earth back into the atmosphere as infrared, or heat, radiation. Most of the infrared energy radiates back out into space, but some of it is absorbed by the trace gases in the atmosphere. The trace-gas molecules warm up, warming the atmosphere.

This process can be compared with the way a greenhouse traps heat inside, keeping the environment warm for plants to grow. A nineteenth-century French scientist named Jean-Baptiste-Joseph Fourier coined the term *greenhouse effect* when he realized that the Earth's atmosphere both allows sunlight to pass through it and heat the Earth's surface and traps radiant heat given off by the Earth.

✳ You have probably experienced the warming effect of gases in the air without realizing it. A clear winter night, though the world outside is beautiful, can be piercingly cold. Add clouds to that scene, and the night might not have such sparkling beauty, but it is warmer because the clouds hold the sun's heat in the troposphere, the lowest level of the atmosphere, where weather occurs.✳

Without the greenhouse effect, Earth's normal temperature would be about 0 degrees F. (-17.8 degrees C)—too cold for life to develop. Instead, the normal temperature of the planet is 59 degrees F. (15 degrees C). If you go deep inside any cavern on earth, you'll find that the temperature is 59 degrees F. (15 degrees C)—a temperature we can live with.

Greenhouse gases do not absorb the infrared rays in sunlight when the light is entering the atmosphere because sunlight is made up of high-frequency, shorter wavelengths, which greenhouse gases cannot absorb. Once the light has struck Earth, however, the soil absorbs it and reradiates it as lower-frequency, long-wavelength, infrared energy, which the greenhouse gases can absorb.

The hotter the body emitting radiation—and the sun is very hot—the shorter are its wavelengths of energy. The short wavelengths are called ultraviolet (UV) rays. Some UV is blocked by an upper level of the atmosphere called the ozone layer. The rest of the sunlight reaches the comparatively cool Earth, which absorbs the heat and reradiates some of it as longer wavelengths of energy.

Any gas with a molecule made up of more than two

ultraviolet reflected by ozone layer

STRATOSPHERE

sunlight absorbed by Earth

OZONE LAYER

GREENHOUSE GASES

TROPOSPHERE

SMOG

sunlight reflected by oceans

infrared rays

trapped heat reflected back

reflected by clouds

sunlight reflected by ice

OCEAN

EARTH

POLAR ICE

17

atoms can absorb infrared. Both nitrogen (N_2) and oxygen (O_2), the main gases of the atmosphere, consist of two atoms. The heat radiation goes right through them. However, carbon dioxide (CO_2), methane (CH_4), ozone (O_3), nitrous oxide (N_2O), and water vapor (H_2O), all have three atoms or more per molecule. Such molecules have the ability to trap heat, warming our planet.

Why is Carbon Dioxide Common?

The periodic table of elements is a special kind of chart showing details about the 103 elements that have been identified as making up the universe. Carbon and oxygen are two of them. The part of the table that includes those two elements is shown below.

Carbon (C) is number 6. Oxygen (O) is number 8 on the table. Notice the row of smaller numbers to the right of each symbol. Carbon has 2 and 4, while oxygen has 2 and 6. These numbers mean that each element has its electrons in two energy rings. Stable atoms need two electrons in the first energy ring, which both elements have. An atom needs 8 electrons in the second ring to be stable. Guess what? The two atoms easily get together and share electrons, thus filling out the second energy ring for each of them. Together they form carbon dioxide.

Can you figure out why the air has N_2 and O_2 instead of just N and O? The chemical formula for ozone is O_3. See if you can find out why three atoms of oxygen hook together in sunlight.

5	2	6	2	7	2	8	2	9	2
B		**C**		**N**		**O**		**F**	
10.811	3	12.01115	4	14.0067	5	15.9994	6	18.9984	7
boron		carbon		nitrogen		oxygen		fluorine	

❋ The Greenhouse Gases

Many gases trap heat, but, like carbon dioxide, the other three main greenhouse gases—methane, nitrous oxide, and ozone—are normal gases in the atmosphere. Some greenhouse gases, however, do not occur naturally on Earth. Called CFCs, they were developed to solve a problem, by scientists who never imagined that these gases would someday create an even greater, global problem. Methane, nitrous oxide, ozone, and CFCs, together, contribute as much to global warming as does carbon dioxide, and their importance is growing. ❋

Carbon Dioxide and Water Vapor. The main greenhouse gas is carbon dioxide, or CO_2—a common gas that is very impor-

Our living world is a balance of plants and animals. Human beings are the only animals that can change that balance.

tant to life. Plants, in the process of photosynthesis, take in carbon dioxide and let out oxygen, keeping the carbon as part of the sugar they need to grow. Animals, in the process of respiration, breathe in the oxygen. It combines with carbon in the body and is exhaled as carbon dioxide. When plants and animals die, the carbon that was in their bodies is released into the soil. New plants grow, absorbing carbon from both soil and air. All the processes together make up a wonderful, balanced system of carbon control for the planet.

But human beings have been changing the equation.

Water vapor is also a greenhouse gas. It works in conjunction with carbon dioxide. When there is a high concentration of CO_2 in the air, the air gets hotter. Additional water evaporates from the oceans because hotter air holds more water vapor than cooler air. Thus the concentration of water vapor in the air rises, trapping more heat and making the air even warmer.

An Earth
Experience

You and Carbon Dioxide

Do humans and other animals add to the carbon dioxide in the atmosphere? Let's run a test on exhaled air. You will first need to prepare a liquid that indicates the presence of carbon dioxide— limewater. Mix a teaspoon of powdered lime, which you can purchase from a garden or farm shop, in a cup of water. Use filter paper in a funnel set in a jar to filter the mixture. The limewater should be clear in the jar. Carbon dioxide will make it become cloudy or milky.

The air around you normally contains 0.03 percent CO_2. Fill a jar half full with limewater. The space above the liquid is filled with air. Cap the jar and shake it so that air bubbles through the limewater. Note that it is still quite clear—0.03 percent isn't very much.

Now blow through a straw into the limewater. It quickly becomes cloudy, indicating that carbon dioxide has been added to the mixture. We breathe out air that is 0.04 percent carbon dioxide. This comes from the breakdown of sugar by every living cell.

Earth currently houses almost 5 billion people, all exhaling carbon dioxide. It has been predicted that more than 3 billion more people will be added during the next forty years.

It will take a lot of plants absorbing carbon dioxide during photosynthesis to handle all that additional CO_2.

Methane gas comes from natural sources, especially the decompo-sition of organic materials when there is no oxygen present, as in rice paddies (left) *and the stomachs of cattle* (above).

Methane. Natural gas is found underground, usually in conjunction with petroleum. It is piped to the surface, where it is used both as a fuel and as a base for other chemicals. About 96 percent of natural gas is the gas called methane (CH_4). Natural gas wells often leak, sending methane into the atmosphere.

The burning of wood and coal also gives off methane. The burning of rain forests in South America and Africa is also producing a great deal of methane.

Methane is not just a fossil fuel formed millions of years ago. Peat bogs are in the process right now of being changed into fuel. If they were left for many millions of years, they would eventually turn into coal, which is why coal is some-times called a renewable resource.

As dead swamp plants gradually turn into peat, they give off methane due to bacterial action underwater. When organic material is decomposed by bacteria without the presence of air (a process called anaerobic decomposition), it gives off methane. Sometimes methane is emitted by the ground in thin streams, which may catch fire. Such methane is often called marsh gas.

Oddly enough, rice paddies give off methane as the rice grows. The amount of land used for rice paddies is increasing because the population is also increasing in countries where rice is the basic food. More than half the world's people depend on rice to live.

Cows and other animals with several stomachs have one stomach where anaerobic bacteria act on the food they chew. These animals continually belch and pass gas, giving off methane each time. Almost 10 percent of everything cows eat turns into methane. About half of all human beings also have similar methane-producing bacteria in their digestive systems. Termites also produce methane. Because termites move into deforested areas, burning the rain forests increases the methane in the atmosphere in a second way.

FACT

There are currently only about 1.7 parts per million of methane in the atmosphere. That doesn't sound like much, but methane is 25 or 30 times better than carbon dioxide at trapping heat, and methane molecules linger in the atmosphere for 7 to 10 years, contributing about 18 percent of global warming. Also, methane is increasing in the atmosphere at a rate of 1 percent per year, faster than any other greenhouse gas.

We can't do much about most methane because it is a result of natural processes, but we can do something about the methane that comes from the landfills where our garbage is dumped. The more organic trash we keep out of landfills by recycling, the less compressed garbage there will be to decompose and give off methane. All landfills should have methane-collection systems that trap the gas and send it to power plants to be used as fuel, instead of just releasing it into the atmosphere.

The numerous cars on our highways put both carbon dioxide and nitrous oxide into the air by burning gasoline.

Nitrous Oxide. Like methane, the gas called nitrous oxide is given off when wood and fossil fuels burn. However, it is also a by-product of a natural process. The air contains nitrogen (N_2). Bacteria in the soil take that nitrogen and convert it first to ammonium (NH_3) and to nitrite (NO_2) and then to nitrate (NO_3), which is a form of nitrogen that plants can use. In the process of that final conversion to nitrate, nitrous oxide (N_2O) is formed.

This, of course, is a process that goes on everywhere, at all times. However, humans encourage the process of adding N_2O to the air by putting nitrogen and ammonium fertilizers on their crops. The nitrous oxide content of the air has gone from 280 parts per billion (not million), before the Industrial Revolution started in the 1700s, to 350 parts per billion now.

Nitrous oxide has been known as "laughing gas" ever since it was first used by a dentist as an anesthetic, but there's nothing laughable about it. Not only does N_2O work to trap heat in the amosphere 250 times better than CO_2, but it also gradually works its way up into the stratosphere where it reacts with ozone, contributing to the loss of the Earth's protective ozone layer. Nitrous oxide stays in the atmosphere about 150 years, and contributes about 6 percent to global warming.

Ozone. Ozone (O_3) is a molecule of three oxygen atoms. It has a slight odor that some people call an "electrical smell." Ozone in the lower atmosphere is the product of sunlight acting on the pollutants that man spews into the air, especially nitrogen oxides from gasoline. On warm, windless days, cities such as Los Angeles put out "ozone alerts," warning people who have lung trouble to stay indoors because the smog is dangerous. Ozone can cause chest pain and throat irritation even in healthy people, and people with health problems can die from bad ozone-filled smogs. Yet, ozone at the upper level of the atmosphere, in the stratosphere, is a lifesaver. The thin layer that collects in the stratosphere prevents dangerous ultraviolet rays in sunlight from reaching the Earth.

CFCs. Chlorofluorocarbons, usually referred to as CFCs, are not natural gases in the atmosphere. They did not exist until the late 1920s, when the Frigidaire Company asked chemist Thomas Midgley of DuPont Company to find a nontoxic substitute for the ammonia and sulfur dioxide used in refrigerators as coolants. Ironically, Midgley also invented leaded gasoline, which is one of the major pollutants of the atmosphere.

Polystyrene foam, also called Styrofoam, is one of the useful items in our society. However, the foam is usually made by expanding liquid plastic with CFCs and other hydrocarbon gases that contribute to global warming and the loss of the ozone layer.

Midgley concocted a new chemical, dichlorodifluoromethane, called CFC-12, which is still the main CFC in use. It is nonreactive, nontoxic, and nonflammable. It not only cools refrigerators and air conditioners but also makes plastic foam expand and propels other chemicals out of aerosol cans. Other varieties of CFCs, as well as related chemicals called halons, were soon found to have many important industrial uses.

CFCs do not easily combine with other chemicals. That is the trait that makes them so useful in aerosol spray cans, and it is also the trait that makes them so dangerous in the atmosphere. Many chemicals put into the air gradually react with oxygen and get cleaned from the air. But CFCs can't be cleaned. They linger and linger, all the time helping to trap heat in the atmosphere and doing it 10,000 times better than carbon dioxide! CFC-11 lasts 75 years in the atmosphere, and CFC-12 lasts 111 years. Just as important, CFCs eventually work their way up into the stratosphere, where they, too, are damaging the ozone layer. We'll see more in Chapter 5 about what happens to CFCs in the ozone layer.

Trapping Heat

Set up this experiment to simulate the effect of the greenhouse effect and global warming. Imagine that a glass jar is the excess carbon dioxide in our atmosphere.

Locate two outdoor thermometers that are the same size and small enough to stand upright in a glass jar. Use modeling clay to hold the thermometers in an upright position about one foot apart. Put these on a table in full sunlight.

Check the temperatures first to be sure the readings are the same. Now turn the glass jar upside down and place it over one thermometer. Every fifteen minutes for an hour, compare the readings of the two thermometers and write down what you see.

Carbon dioxide and the other gases work somewhat like the glass jar or greenhouse windows. They form a blanket around the Earth that keeps heat from escaping into space.

Where the Gases Come From

Most greenhouse gases are created when we burn fossil fuels—coal, oil, and natural gas—for energy. All the carbon that was bound up in the fuel is released during burning, and it forms carbon dioxide with the oxygen in the air.

A gallon (3.7 liters) of liquid gasoline weighs about 7 pounds (3 kilograms). But when it is burned in a car, it produces about 20 pounds (9 kilograms) of carbon dioxide. And more cars are driven longer distances in America each year than in all other nations put together!

A kilowatt-hour of electricity produced by a power plant using coal for its fuel puts 2 pounds (0.9 kilogram) of CO_2

into the atmosphere. That amount comes from a chunk not much larger than the one shown in the illustration. One 100-watt electric bulb left running after you get home from school until midnight uses about one kilowatt-hour of electricity.

A large jet flying from Montreal, Canada, to San Francisco, California—a distance of about 2,500 miles (4,000 kilometers)— will produce about 125 tons (112 metric tons) of carbon dioxide.

Such activities go on all the time in North America—activities that we take for granted. And they add to the greenhouse gases in the atmosphere.

Coal taken from the Earth has been the basic fuel used by industrial nations to develop their businesses and industries. Just when Third World nations are hoping to use their own coal supplies to industrialize, we have learned that the burning of coal is endangering our planet.

Each man, woman, and child in America adds 20 tons (18 metric tons) of carbon dioxide to the atmosphere each year. Canadians are almost as bad—at about 17 tons (15 metric tons) per person. Australia is next highest with 16 tons (14.5 metric tons). The smallest addition is from the African nation of Zaire, which adds only about 200 pounds (90 kilograms) per person per year—that's the equivalent of three short automobile trips for a North American!

Americans put about 25 percent of the excess CO_2 into the atmosphere, though we have less than 5 percent of the world's population. The leading source of CO_2 (about 32 percent) is power plants burning fossil fuels for electricity.

The second main source, 29 percent, is transportation, primarily automobiles. The United States has approximately

Power plants that generate electricity are the main source of emissions that spew greenhouse gases into the atmosphere.

150 million cars, while China has less than a million! Unfortunately, the car has become the symbol of the good life in America and around the world. Also unfortunately, a passenger car emits CO_2 equal to its own weight every year!

The third major source is industry, 23 percent. Of course, a lot of industry also runs on electricity, generated by the first most important source, power plants.

Household use of fossil fuels accounts for 14 percent. Heating, hot water, and electricity for homes are one category that the average North American can do something

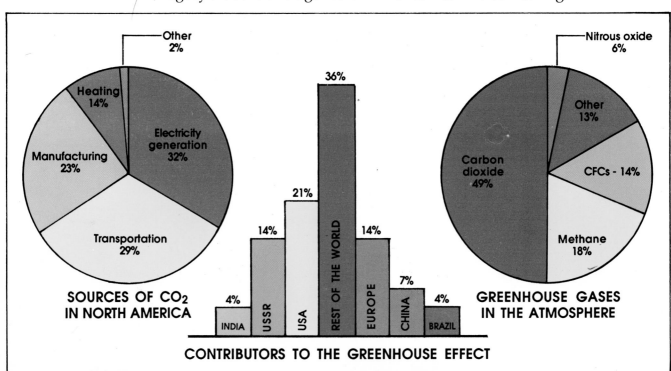

SOURCES OF CO_2 IN NORTH AMERICA

- Other 2%
- Heating 14%
- Electricity generation 32%
- Manufacturing 23%
- Transportation 29%

CONTRIBUTORS TO THE GREENHOUSE EFFECT

- INDIA 4%
- USSR 14%
- USA 21%
- REST OF THE WORLD 36%
- EUROPE 14%
- CHINA 7%
- BRAZIL 4%

GREENHOUSE GASES IN THE ATMOSPHERE

- Nitrous oxide 6%
- Other 13%
- CFCs - 14%
- Carbon dioxide 49%
- Methane 18%

about. In China, the growth of industry is officially more important than providing power to homes, so most residences in rural areas get no electric power during the day.

Until it joined West Germany and began to fix up its factories, East Germany was the only nation in the world to produce more CO_2 per person than the United States. Worldwide, an average of 3.88 tons (3.5 metric tons) per person per year is produced.

Obviously, most excess CO_2 comes from human activities. And it's only humans who can do something to stop the global warming.

Walter Broecker, an oceanographer at Columbia University, wrote in *Nature:* "The inhabitants of planet Earth are quietly conducting a gigantic environmental experiment. So vast and sweeping will be the consequences that, were it brought before any responsible council for approval, it would be firmly rejected."

The eruption of a volcano, such as Mount St. Helens in Washington state, spews huge quantities of heat and gases into the atmosphere. But no amount of volcanic action can damage the atmosphere as much as humans have.

The CO_2 You Add to the Atmosphere

You can make an estimate of how many pounds of CO_2 you add to the atmosphere in a week.

Record how many car trips you make and the distance you travel. If a trip was just for your benefit—perhaps to go home late from football practice—count the whole trip for yourself. If your family goes together, divide the distance driven among the members of your family. Divide the distance for the week by the miles per gallon your car gets and multiply that answer by 20 to learn how many pounds of CO_2 your driving adds to the air.

Ask to see your family's electric bill. It should show how many kilowatt-hours (kWh) were used over how many days. Find the number of kWh for one week and divide it by the number of people in your family. Multiply that by 2 pounds to get your total. If you're not sure whether your power company burns coal, call and ask. If your company uses nuclear power or power generated by a dam, your electricity adds no CO_2 to the atmosphere.

Find out how your home or apartment is heated. If the heating system is electrical, it will be in the electric bill. If your system uses natural gas, look at your heating bill. It will show the number of therms (a unit of heat) used for a certain number of days. Again, divide by four and then by the number of people in your family.

If you take a trip by air, you need to add the total of the distance you traveled multiplied by 1/2 pound.

Of course, goods and services you buy require power. Double your total to get indirect CO_2 you produce. That figure is your total for the week. Multiply that figure by 52 weeks to get your total for the year. How did your total compare to the average American or Canadian?

Deforestation. Although motor vehicles and power plants account for nearly 75 percent of the carbon dioxide pollution from industrialized nations, the cutting and burning of tropical forests is also a major contributor. In many developing countries along the equator, rain forests and their jungles are viewed as problems to be disposed of instead of as natural resources to be preserved. When a Malaysian burns 1 acre (0.4 hectare) of rain forest in order to clear it for cattle grazing, 200 tons (180 metric tons) of carbon dioxide, as well as methane and nitrous oxide, spew into the air.

The greenhouse gases are put into the air over the burning forest, but winds come along and carry them up into the atmosphere. There, global winds pick them up and carry them through the troposphere around the planet. And the damage doesn't stop there.

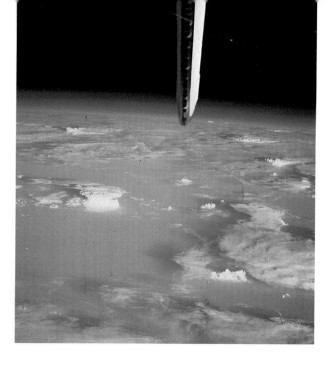

A photograph taken by astronauts aboard the space shuttle Discovery *reveals great plumes of smoke billowing from a perpetual white haze caused by the burning of rain forests in South America.*

Farmers around the world burn their fields to prepare them for new planting. The burning of any plant matter adds carbon dioxide to the atmosphere.

31

Clear-cutting of large blocks of forests, such as these in the United States, eliminates millions of trees from the Earth-saving work of absorbing carbon dioxide from the air.

The great green canopies of the rain forest have the ability to remove large quantities of carbon dioxide, ozone, and nitrous oxide from the air. Without such forests, global warming will become worse. Also, the soil under the Amazon rain forests contains a great deal of nitrous oxide. When the soil is disturbed by turning it over for pasture and farmland, it releases that nitrous oxide, again adding to the global warming.

Cutting down forests is not just a tropical activity. The world is losing forestland at the rate of 1 acre (0.4 hectare) *per second*. The U.S. government is allowing so much cutting in old forests that there may be none left in twenty years. Canada, too, is cutting down its great western rain forests at an alarming rate.

Decomposers and Carbon Dioxide

A vital part of all food chains in ecosystems are the decomposers. Lacking chlorophyll, these organisms—fungi and bacteria—must get their energy by breaking down dead plants and animals. In the process, a lot of carbon dioxide is released.

Purchase a package of dry yeast at the grocery store. Yeast is a fungus that feeds on sugar. Even though the package you buy appears to contain a dry powder, that powder is really tiny one-celled plants that are still alive but in a dormant stage.

Ask an adult to help you with this activity.

Dissolve some sugar in half a cup of warm (not boiling) water. Add a small amount of yeast. The yeast plants immediately become active in the warmth and moisture. They grow and reproduce as they break down the sugar into alcohol and carbon dioxide.

Carefully hold a lighted match near the surface of the mixture. What happens to the flame? Do you know why?

Decomposition is occurring all the time on the floor of a forest, in the bottom of the ocean, on the ground of a prairie, and in the mud of a marsh. This is a normal and necessary process in nature. When humans upset the balance in these communities, by cutting down a tropical rain forest, for example, decomposition occurs at faster rates, putting even more CO_2 into the atmosphere.

How We Got Here

Throughout much of Earth's history, the temperature of the planet was warmer than it is today, perhaps 25 degrees F.

Except around the coasts, Greenland has been bound up in glaciers and ice since medieval times. It could warm up again if global warming continues.

years ago, most of the land was tropical, even as far north as Alaska. The air was heavy with moisture.

Then the Earth began to cool. More and more of the planet's water was locked up in ice. Great sheets of ice, many miles thick, covered most of the polar regions. The dinosaurs were already becoming extinct when, many scientists say, something dramatic happened that lowered the average global temperature even further for a long, long time. Then, it began to gradually rise again.

About 150,000 years ago, the temperature began to drop again. It settled at an average global temperature about 9 degrees F. (5 degrees C) cooler than our temperature today. But that difference was enough to make glaciers 2 miles (3 kilometers) thick that moved down and over much of North

America and Europe. Many species of plants and animals were able to make their way south and wait out the glacial period, though many others were unable to migrate and became extinct. When the region began to warm again, and the glaciers retreated, some made their way north again.

This glaciation happened four times over the last million years. Each time, living things were dislocated—many species disappeared forever, while others changed location and never returned. The last ice age melted enough to open up the Northern Hemisphere to human habitation, and civilization began to develop about 10,000 years ago.

About a thousand years ago, the North Atlantic warmed up again, ice melted, and the Norsemen were able to sail to a warm, green, and fertile island they called Greenland. We find that name startling today because it means that the island was far different from the icebound land we know now. While the Norse colonies flourished there—briefly—stalwart sailors such as Leif Ericson may well have sailed down into what is now the United States.

At approximately the same time, American Indians of the northern Great Plains found their bountiful climate changing to a permanent drought. They died out or moved away. The Pueblo Indians of Mesa Verde also moved, abandoning their cliffside "apartment" complexes. From then on, the Plains Indians lived nomadic lives, moving with the seasons.

The period called the Little Ice Age began about 1400 and lasted until about 1800. People in Greenland starved to death because they could not grow crops. The River Thames in England froze over each winter. Even the Baltic Sea froze. Forests were cut down for firewood and never replanted. The climate was unpredictable. Sometimes the growing season was warm enough to produce a decent crop. Other times it wasn't, and famine struck.

These warm and cool periods, which had a major effect on human living conditions, occurred because the average global temperature rose or fell by probably not more than 2 degrees F. (less than 1 degree C). On a warm summer day, you wouldn't even notice such a change in the temperature. But when a drop in temperature happens all over the globe at the same time —and stays that way—such a change increases the number of days below freezing and shortens the growing season.

These changes in the global environment were among the natural fluctuations of our planet, but for the last two hundred years a new factor has come into play. Humans, instead of just being among the species affected by climate change, are themselves changing Earth's climate.

Human Industry. As the Little Ice Age was ending, northern Europeans began to prosper. They raised larger families, and the population grew. Machines started to be used on farms, machines that had to be made in factories. And so the number of factories grew, too. However, they ran into a problem. The European forests had been cut down during the long cold period, and factories could not get enough wood to make all the charcoal they needed. They had to start using coal for fuel to run the factories.

Coal is basically fossilized carbon. It was deposited in the Earth during the Carboniferous Age, about 250 million years ago. At that time, Earth was covered with huge tropical swamps. When plants died, they fell into the water and did not completely decompose. Instead, they turned into peat,

The availability of coal-produced electricity allowed craftsmen such as these carpenters to accomplish much more work than they had been able to do by hand. However, our Earth is now paying the price for a society dependent on fossil fuels to run machines.

which was later covered by soil and rock and compressed.

Coal itself isn't just compressed carbon, however. It contains lots of contaminants—extra gases that make it smelly and smoky, and cause it to burn unpredictably. So people did not like to use it.

Then an Englishman from Shropshire named Abraham Darby discovered that he could make coal into coke in much the same way as charcoal is made from wood. He partially burned coal in a closed oven. Because oxygen can't get to the coal, its gases are driven off by the heat, but the coal itself is not burned. When coke was used to make iron products, the iron produced was always of the same quality.

Suddenly there was a huge demand for coke, and coal mining turned into a great, new, international business. Steam power became possible. The Industrial Revolution had begun. Coal quickly became—and remains—the main fuel used by industry all over the world.

There is enough coal left on Earth to continue using it at the same rate for several hundred years. But most scientists think that disaster caused by global warming will strike us long before the fossil fuel supply is used up.

Chapter 3

Scientists
at Work

Scientists have spent many years studying the movement of the atmosphere in specific areas. For example, they can pretty well predict the movement of a hurricane from the equator where these huge storms are born, through the Caribbean Sea, and up the eastern coast of the United States. They can warn residents in the storm's path to batten down the hatches or escape to safety.

But predicting what will happen globally is another matter entirely. We have just recently come to grips with the concept that Earth is a single entity that must be looked at as a whole. We are just beginning to learn about how small changes in one area can affect the whole planet. There is some evidence, for example, that the strength of hurricanes in the Caribbean depends on the amount of rainfall in a desert area of western Africa called the Sahel.

The greenhouse effect was discovered in 1896 by Swedish chemist Svante Arrhenius in his efforts to learn why the atmosphere stays warm when oxygen and nitrogen, the two main atmospheric gases, do not absorb heat. Arrhenius discovered that traces of carbon dioxide in the atmosphere were responsible. He even recognized that human activities were adding to the effect, though he thought it would be completely beneficial. After all, the greenhouse effect makes life possible on Earth.

The greenhouse effect is also the reason why life is *not* possible on the planet Venus. Venus is 26 million miles (42 million kilometers) closer to the sun than Earth is. The average global temperature on Earth is 59 degrees F. (15 degrees C). The average temperature on Venus is more than 800 degrees F. (430 degrees C)! The difference between the two

planets does not come from Venus being closer to the sun than Earth. Instead, it comes from the heavy cloud layer on Venus that lets the sun's rays through to the planet's surface but does not let the heat rays back out. Venus's atmosphere is 98 percent CO_2. Earth's atmosphere contains only 0.03 percent CO_2, and yet that figure, too, is beginning to rise, and the planet is getting warmer.

The atmosphere of Venus contains more than three thousand times more carbon dioxide than Earth's. The runaway greenhouse effect raises the temperature so high that life could not exist.

Measuring Carbon Dioxide

As the amount of carbon dioxide in the atmosphere rises, the average global temperature rises, too. The amount of change observed so far—a rise of 25 percent since 1800—comes from the addition of only 70 molecules of CO_2 per million molecules of air!

The existence of carbon dioxide in the air was first discovered by Scottish scientist David Black in 1754. But it was well over one hundred years before scientists could measure it precisely. Even after that, however, the recorded measurements were made randomly and by different procedures. So no one knows how valid the written records are.

In 1938, G. D. Callendar, an English engineer, matched the long-term temperature rise with the long-term increase in carbon dioxide in the atmosphere, but no one was particularly impressed. He thought that global warming would be completely advantageous because plants grow better when there is more CO_2 in the atmosphere.

The keeping of exact, daily records began in 1958, when David Keeling, a student at California's Scripps Institute of

Oceanography, went to live at Hawaii's Mauna Loa Observatory. Keeling's records were related to a major study on the exchange of carbon dioxide between the air and the sea. The professors who sent Keeling to Hawaii had discovered that the ocean absorbed less carbon dioxide than expected, and they suggested that it may have been entering the atmosphere and warming the planet. They wrote, "Within a few centuries we are returning to the atmosphere and oceans the concentrated organic carbon stored in the sedimentary rocks over hundreds of millions of years."

Keeling has watched the concentration of carbon dioxide go up and down with the seasons and even with longer term fluctuations. But always, the baseline level of CO_2 has risen. His first measurements at Mauna Loa revealed a CO_2 concentration of 315 parts per million (ppm), higher than any previously recorded readings. Few scientists saw reason to get concerned about the increase. No one was sure what the number meant until, in the mid-1980s, scientists analyzed air that had been trapped in ice about the time of the Industrial Revolution. They learned that in 1800 there was a carbon dioxide concentration of 280 ppm. In 1989, the figure was 354 ppm, and half of the increase has taken place since 1960.

Studies show that it takes 2.13 billion tons (1.9 billion metric tons) of carbon added to the air for the CO_2 level to

The Mauna Loa Observatory is 11,000 feet (3.3 kilometers) up on a dormant volcano, far above man-made sources of pollution. It is even above the tree line, so that plants can't add to the carbon dioxide being measured.

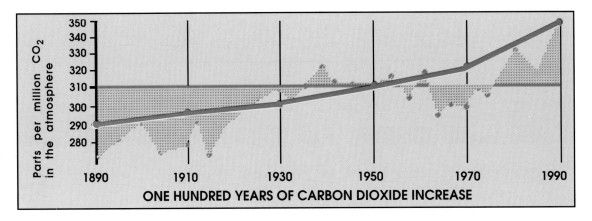

$$\text{Parts per million } CO_2 \text{ in the atmosphere}$$

350
340
330
320
310
300
290
280

1890   1910   1930   1950   1970   1990

ONE HUNDRED YEARS OF CARBON DIOXIDE INCREASE

On top of the graph that shows rising global temperatures in the last hundred years, which was described on page 11, a bold line shows the increase in carbon dioxide in the atmosphere over the same period of time. Temperatures and CO_2 concentration have followed each other up and down for thousands of years.

rise by 1 ppm. According to one estimate, human activities have put more carbon into the air since 1800 than is contained in all the living things on the planet.

Studying Ice Cores

Hans Oeschger, a Swiss physicist, developed the idea of giving climate scientists "fossil air" to study, the way a paleontologist studies fossil animals. The only place the fossil air could be found was in ice. In 1971, scientists from the Soviet Union began drilling a hole in the thick ice of East Antarctica. The drill bit was hollow, so that it brought ice up into the tube as it turned. Foot by foot, for fourteen years, the workers added more tube and the drill went deeper. Finally, in 1985, the drill was removed, and a tubular core of ice was removed that was more than 1 mile (2 kilometers) long. Called the Vostok Core, it was cut into 7-inch (18-centimeter) sections and quickly bagged to prevent contamination. The sections were flown to refrigerated laboratories in France where scientists come from all over the world to study them.

The ice core contains samples of ice formed year after year, century after century, going back 160,000 years. As

Antarctic snow freezes into ice, tiny bubbles of air are trapped. Scientists can analyze the bubbles in the ice core, inch by inch, and discover what the air was like at any particular time.

The main thing the scientists have learned from the ice core is that the carbon dioxide content of the air has risen and fallen through the ages along with temperature. There was less CO_2 (down to 180 ppm) during the Ice Ages. There was more (up to 280 ppm) during the warm interglacial periods.

Similar ice cores from Greenland showed the same readings, so we know that the CO_2 level changes were global. And we know that never, in 160,000 years, have the CO_2 levels been as high as they are now!

The air trapped in an ice core is released in a glass jar from which all other air has been removed. The gases in the "fossil air" can then be analyzed. They show what the atmosphere was like at the time the ice was formed.

Mathematical Models of the Atmosphere

Scientists have long used mathematical models of the Earth's atmosphere to show "what would happen if . . ." They give numbers to all the different aspects that they can measure, such as temperature of the ocean, days of sunlight, percentage of cloud cover. These are very simple models that assume that the atmosphere is the same all over the globe, which, of course, is not true.

Recently, scientists using very powerful computers have developed models based on global circulation of the atmosphere. These models assume that the atmosphere is three-dimensional. They include what we know about the laws of physics as well as scientists' assumptions on heat emission

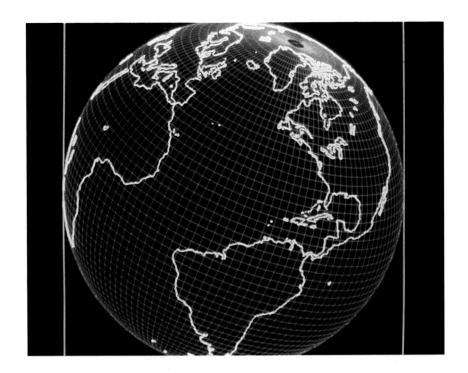

Very detailed models of the atmosphere have a three-dimensional grid covering the planet. Measurements are put in for spots 400 miles (640 kilometers) apart all over the globe, plus nine different layers up through the atmosphere. Computers have to deal with measurements at 20,000 different locations. Each model has to run about 200,000 equations—but that still is not enough to give scientists much detail.

by the ground, atmospheric convection, soil moisture, ocean currents, sea ice, and clouds. They can mathematically change one factor and see the effect on the others.

The scientists wanted to discover what factor would raise the temperature of areas at the same latitudes as North America to the level reached during the hot, wet Cretaceous Period when dinosaurs lived. They found that the only way to get such an increase in temperature was to add carbon dioxide to the atmosphere.

One of the important factors that scientists test is the continuing increase of carbon dioxide in the atmosphere. They agree that if CO_2 emissions continue at their current rate, the planet's average global temperature will rise about 5.4 degrees F. (3 degrees C) by the year 2050. What they can't agree on is what the politicians want to know: How will such a rise affect *my* country, *my* state, *my* farmers' fields?

The area made by a square of the grid in the best models is about the size of California, and certainly California has a vast number of differences in climate, depending on such factors as the nearness of the ocean, elevation of the mountains, and presence of desert. Few of the variables deal with the effects of the oceans and the formation of clouds, because we don't know enough about those two elements.

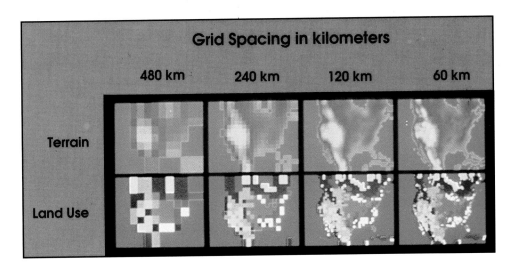

One model used by the National Center for Atmospheric Research shows terrain and land use with details at 298 miles (480 kilometers) (far left). Each time the size of the grid is halved, a great deal more detail is shown.

If scientists tried to increase the details in the models by a factor of 10 (put readings in for every 40 miles [64 kilometers] instead of every 400 miles [640 kilometers]), the models would have to be run on a computer a thousand times more powerful than the supercomputers now being used! Even then, the results would still be an estimate because Earth is so much more complicated than any computer program we can create.

Science and Politics

Scientists have been reporting their findings on global warming to those people who would listen ever since David Keeling's CO_2 measurements were announced. But most people felt that the increase had nothing to do with them and, if it was important, someone else would deal with it someday.

In 1980, for the first time, a conference was held to discuss what the greenhouse effect could mean to public policy instead of just to science. The scientists pointed out that only government action would make people cut down on the use of the fossil fuels that were pouring greenhouse gases into the atmosphere.

Three years later, a study by the United States Environmental Protection Agency (EPA) was released which said that it was already too late to do anything to stop a major warming trend and that people should be looking into ways to adapt to a warmer world. The public began to become concerned.

Still the U.S. Congress did not really listen until June 23, 1988, when Dr. James Hansen, director of NASA's Goddard Institute of Space Studies, testified that "global warming is now sufficiently large that we can ascribe with a high degree of confidence a cause and effect relationship to the greenhouse effect. . . ." Even as he spoke, Washington, D.C., was sweltering in a heat wave. North America was experiencing the warmest year on record. At last, people began to listen.

Most scientists were predicting at that time that global warming would become a major problem by the middle of the 21st century. General agreement was that the present rate of emissions, plus the rate of growth that already exists,

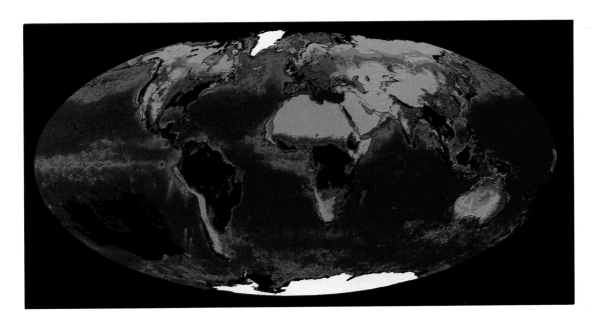

would lead to a rise of 1.8 to 5.4 degrees F. (1 to 3 degrees C) by 2030. However, in October 1990 scientists said that the average global temperature must not be allowed to rise more than 0.2 of 1 degree F. (0.1 of 1 degree C) per decade—or a maximum of 0.8 degree F. (0.44 degree C)—if catastrophic events were to be avoided. One of the main reasons was the possibility that a more rapid increase could cause sudden and unpredictable jumps in climate change. The current rate of change, if it continues, is *three times faster* than the acceptable rate!

NASA has chosen to study the question of global warming with one of the biggest space projects yet—the Earth Observing System (EOS). This system of environmental satellites would provide 15 years' worth of data for scientists to use in improving their mathematical models and for increasing understanding of two of the biggest unknowns—clouds and oceans. But the first orbiting observation platform is not scheduled for launch until 1997, and the world needs answers before then.

NASA's Nimbus 7 satellite provided years of data that allowed scientists to create this map of Earth's biosphere, or plant life. Red and orange in the oceans show the concentration of phytoplankton, the microscopic plants at the base of the food chain. Shades of green show forests and grasslands, while yellow regions are barren. Global warming could change both the quality and the location of plant life.

What We Don't Know

Few elected officials want to be the ones to tell the public that they must cut their driving in half or turn off their air conditioners, so many prefer to listen to those scientists who are not in total agreement that global warming is taking place. They emphasize the possibility that it might stop even if we don't take action, just as climate shifts have reversed themselves in the past. For example, in recent years—from about 1940 to 1970—there was a slight cooling of the average global temperature. Maybe the current warming is a trend that will reverse itself again.

Despite the general agreement that warming is happening, we still don't know enough about some questions.

Feedbacks. Some factors in the atmosphere can enhance the effects of the greenhouse gases or subtract from them. Those that strengthen the warming are called "positive feedbacks." Those that would tend to keep the Earth cooler are called "negative feedbacks."

Water vapor is a powerful, positive feedback, increasing the warming effect of the greenhouse gases. The warmer the atmosphere, the more water evaporates, increasing the greenhouse effect and thus evaporating even more water. However, some scientists think that water vapor has a negative feedback near the equator. They think that the rising columns of moist air give up their moisture as rain, thus creating a dry atmosphere above the columns of air. So the total effect is one of drying and cooling the atmosphere.

The Question of Clouds. Clouds can be positive or negative feedbacks, depending on their altitude. Clouds are one

of the most puzzling factors in global warming.

Low-lying stratocumulus clouds, especially over oceans, decrease global warming because they reflect the heat from the sun. On the other hand, high icy cirrus clouds increase the effect. The sunlight goes through them, but the heat rays, going the other direction, do not. Since 1986, a major study of clouds has been going on in order to increase the accuracy of the cloud factor in global climate models.

Clouds are also increased through the addition of sulfur dioxide to the atmosphere. Sulfur dioxide is a pollutant from burning that is blamed for acid rain. However, increased cloud cover may explain why temperatures have not risen in industrial areas as much as was projected. Perhaps we should not worry about emissions from smokestacks.

Other Questions. We know that Earth's atmosphere has had different amounts of carbon dioxide in it at various times in history. But we don't know what caused those changes before humans came along and changed things. Is there some mechanism related to the sun, or to rock weathering, or some other factor we don't know about?

Scientists have long known that the oceans are one of the main carbon "sinks"—they store a great deal of carbon dioxide. They also can store one thousand times as much heat as the atmosphere can! That means that even though the atmosphere itself might not warm as much as predicted, the ocean will get warm enough to inundate the land anyway.

Scientists need to learn more about how and when water vapor condenses to droplets and forms a cloud. Global warming would mean more clouds in the sky. But clouds reflect sunlight, so they might have the effect of cooling the Earth.

Temperature differences at different places on the Earth's surface make the atmosphere circulate. Currently there is a great deal of difference between the polar regions and the equator, making vast wind currents that circulate through the atmosphere of each hemisphere. If those differences are evened out, as is predicted, there might not be as much air circulation. We don't know what that would mean.

As the lower atmosphere warms, more heat is drawn from the upper stratosphere, 25 miles (40 kilometers) high. Scientists have found that the temperature of the stratosphere has already dropped 3.5 to 5.5 degrees F. (2 to 3 degrees C) in the last ten years. They don't know how important that fact is.

One of the biggest unknowns involves the computer models used for predicting global warming. Because there are still many things not known about our planet, the modelers had to make assumptions about certain factors. We have no way of knowing how accurate those assumptions are. The people who have debunked the idea of global warming think the assumptions are grossly wrong.

According to Peter Rogers of Harvard University, only 60 percent of the CO_2 put into the atmosphere over the last 100

Earth's vast oceans remain a mystery. Scientists need to learn more about the way they absorb carbon dioxide and hold heat.

About 20,000 years ago, so much water was bound up in glacial ice that the oceans were 400 feet lower. For example, the Gulf of Mexico was much smaller.

The glaciers melted and the sea rose. The waters of the Gulf of Mexico spread, swallowing up much of the land around it.

years through fossil-fuel use and burning has remained in the atmosphere. Where has all that CO_2 gone? Likewise, why hasn't the average global temperature risen as much as the models say it should have, considering the amount of fuel burned? We don't know.

The only way we can know for sure whether the global temperature will continue rising is to live through the next decades. Each day we will have more information to use in making up our minds. Maybe it will turn out that we'll keep adding greenhouse gases to the atmosphere but the upward trend in temperatures will cease. Then some scientists will be able to say, "We told you so." But, more likely, it will turn out that the temperature will keep rising, and each day we will have less chance to change our behavior. But by then it will be too late to change the effects. We will have to live in a world very different from the one we know now.

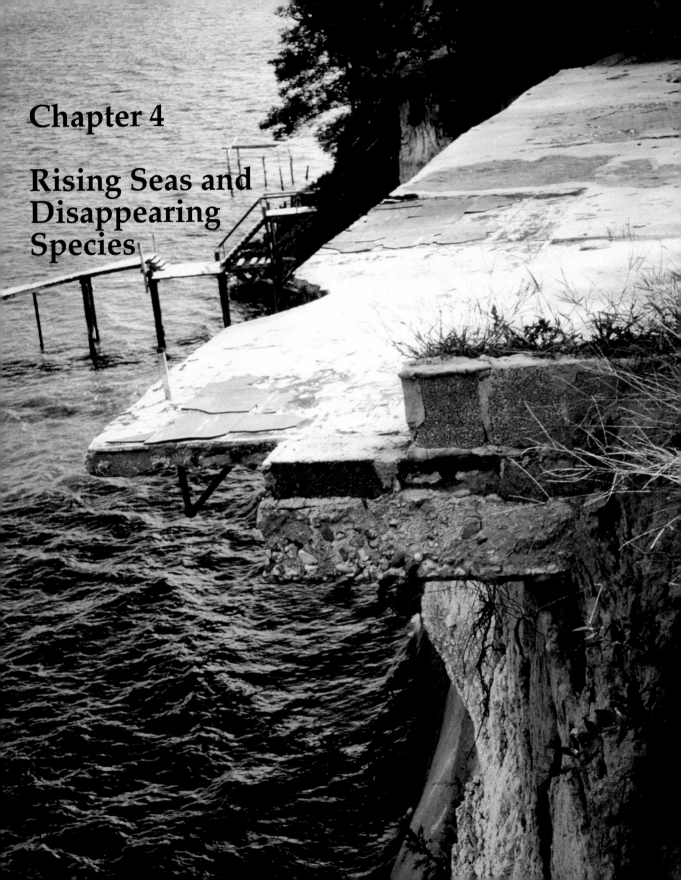

Chapter 4

Rising Seas and Disappearing Species

The one thing that most scientists agree on at this time is that the average global temperature is rising. Exactly what this means to us as individuals and to Earth as a habitat is still uncertain, though reasonable guesses can be made.

The major categories of predicted effect are: 1) a rise in the level of the sea, 2) loss of plant and animal species, and 3) climate change, especially in the temperate regions of the Northern and Southern Hemispheres. These effects are, of course, interrelated.

None of the effects is going to be so clean-cut that we can directly blame global warming. Acid rain, ozone depletion, and air pollution buildup in the troposphere are all being stirred in an unpredictable witch's cauldron. They are all interrelated and, fortunately, they can all be tackled at once. If we work on fixing one, we work on fixing them all.

Two-Faced Changes

Some changes stemming from the major effects may be beneficial to people, some may not. Most changes will probably be two-faced—they will bring benefits for some places on the Earth and difficulties for others.

For example, one effect that most scientists agree on is that in northern latitudes, winters will become less severe. That may sound wonderful for people who have to bundle up through the dark, cold months, but there are several less beneficial aspects. Without major snowfalls in the mountains, there will be no melting snow in spring to fill the water reservoirs of such heavily populated areas as Los Angeles, California.

Another penalty is that if winter is warmer, summer is

warmer, too. Cities that now have only one or two 100-degree F. (38-degree C) days each summer will have eighteen or twenty. A 1989 study found that if global warming continues unabated, at least 86 more power plants will be required across the United States just to power the air conditioners that would be needed during the hottest days. And the power plants would need to burn more fossil fuel, making global warming worse.

The difficulty with such two-faced changes is that scientists cannot predict just which effects will touch what locations or to what extent. They cannot say that Chicago, Illinois, will have 25 more days above 90 degrees F. (32 degrees C) while Toronto, Canada, will have only 20 more, or that Tucson, Arizona, which regularly has temperatures above 110 degrees F. (44 degrees C) will become unbearable. These are things governments and politicians want to know, but for which there are no answers.

Sea-Level Rise

It is predicted that the level of the ocean against the land will rise as the Earth warms. This happens for two reasons: the water itself expands as it gets warmer—thermal expansion—and warmer temperatures melt the glaciers in the mountains and in Greenland, so that huge quantities of additional water are dumped into the oceans.

If the warming is allowed to go unchecked, the sea could be at least 3 feet (90 centimeters) higher one hundred years from now. And 225,000 miles (362,250 kilometers) of coastline around the world would be uninhabitable. Half of all human beings live in coastal regions, and 15 of the world's 20 largest cities would be affected by sea-level rise.

The sea is already rising. Some Canadian scientists have analyzed the records of sea-level measurements made all over the world during the last hundred years. Removing the local effects and probable incorrect measurements, they still came up with a rise of 1/10 of an inch (2.5 millimeters) per year, or perhaps as much as 6 inches (15 centimeters) average rise around the world. The ocean rose 12 inches (30 centimeters) on the Atlantic coast of North America, because of the additional effect of eastern shores sinking. Since 1958, a rise in temperature of almost 1 degree F. (0.5 degree C) has taken place in the deep oceans. Such a warming will not easily go away.

Many beach houses are built on stilts to keep them out of the tidal waters. But if sea level rises permanently, not even stilts will pro-tect such houses from the water. Some states are prohibiting houses from being built on ocean shores.

Molecules on the Move

Will a given amount of cool water take up more room if it is warmed? Let's find out.

Locate a 1-quart (or 1-liter) jar with a screw-on lid. Put the lid upside down on a piece of wood and carefully hammer a small nail through the center to make a hole. Set the jar and lid in the refrigerator for several hours to get it very cold.

Fill a 2-quart (or 2-liter) pitcher with water and ice. Stir until the water is icy. Then pour the water, but no ice, into the cold quart jar until it is full to the brim. Using an eye dropper or a teaspoon, add water until it is ready to overflow. Slowly screw on the lid. If any water comes out of the hole, wipe it off with a towel.

Set the jar aside until it warms up to room temperature. Note any water that may come out of the hole as the temperature rises. Place the jar in a pan full of hot water. Does more water come out of the hole?

Since you didn't add any more water to the jar, what can you conclude about what was happening to the water?

As molecules are heated, they begin to bounce around, taking up more room than before. This is called thermal expansion.

Expanding Water. At first it seems as if a warming world would have higher water levels simply because the glaciers would melt. However, the main reason for higher shorelines is the fact that water expands when it gets warm. Also, if surface water warms, ocean currents are likely to be affected. Ocean currents play a major role in the development of the great fishing beds on which the world depends for food. If

the currents change, the food supplies for people could easily change, too.

When water expands, it requires more room. The rocky sea bottom and continental coasts won't move to make room, so the water can only go higher, causing problems for life on the shore, or even destroying the shore itself. If the sea-level rise is rapid, low-lying coral islands, for example, may be flooded. This would not be a temporary flood that could be survived. It would be a permanent change.

The Maldives are a chain of 1,190 beautiful coral islands in the Indian Ocean near India. Only about 200 of them are populated, with a total of about 200,000 people. A rise in the sea of only 6 feet (2 meters) would cover their homeland.

Add Some Ice. Most of the Earth's fresh water is tied up in the polar ice caps and glaciers. If the planet gets warmer, some of that ice must melt. The water released by the melting will contribute to the sea-level rise. In addition, as ice melts, icebergs would probably break off in greater numbers, endangering shipping. They would be so huge that they would not have melted before reaching the latitudes where floating oil rigs are located.

Actually, the ice melt is already happening. One scientist has measured ice thickness in the Arctic and found that about 55 cubic miles (217 cubic kilometers) of ice disappeared from a Nevada-sized section of the Arctic over an eleven-year period. An English researcher found that the Arctic ice, especially in Greenland, has lost more than 2 1/2 feet (75 centimeters) of depth in the last thirteen years.

Polar ice has melted before in Earth's history. Scientists have evidence that about 95,000 years ago a chunk of the Antarctic ice sheet broke off that was so big the oceans rose many feet. Perhaps that rise was the source of the story of Noah's flood in the Bible.

The West Antarctic Ice Sheet is an incredibly huge ice sheet that sits on land below sea level. If the water around it warms very much, it is so unstable that it might break apart. It would enter the warmer water and melt, possibly raising the water by as much as 9 feet (2.7 meters). This would flood not just the low-lying coastal regions, but also deep inland areas. Although it would probably take several hundred years to happen, such ice breakage and melting would mean that numerous islands around the world would disappear.

The ice-bound continent of Antarctica holds vast amounts of the Earth's water. If global warming continues, much of that water could eventually be released into the seas, raising the level of the oceans all over the world. However, Antarctica is so cold that even a warming of several degrees may cause little melting.

People in Danger. The island of Manhattan in New York City, surrounded by the At-lantic Ocean, the Hudson River, and the East River, is the most populated island in the world. That city would need to spend many millions of dollars to build levees that would hold back the tides. Otherwise, the city would be swamped by tides twice each day.

Low-lying coastal regions of many populated countries would also become unusable. Wealthy countries might be able to build enough dikes to keep the water back from major cities, but poor countries such as Bangladesh would be unable to do that. Much of Bangladesh is, on the average, only about 10 feet (3 meters) above sea level. Some scientists have predicted that as many as 46 million people would be forced out of Bangladesh and Egypt alone.

Where would all those people go? There is considerable evidence from history that residents of an area become angry when a large number of newcomers move in. They become afraid that the newcomers will take their jobs, use up their food, buy up their land, bring in new diseases. Sometimes wars start when populations begin to shift. The refugee problem would not be easy to solve.

Wetland Loss. In addition to cities and their people, much of our land would be affected. It has been estimated that if the oceans rise 3 feet (90 centimeters), the United States could lose three-fourths of its wetlands, mostly in the Mississippi Delta. Most scientists think that it is already too late to stop a 3-foot rise.

Both Long Island (the big island on the right) and Manhattan Island (shown between rivers at the west end of Long Island) are low-lying, very populated areas. The rising sea would cover Manhattan Island, flooding its subways and streets if unprotected by massive levees. One of the major business capitals of the world would come to a standstill.

Wetlands are marshes and lagoons that flood part or all of the year. Their water is rich in nutrients that support numerous living things. Coastal wetlands, such as the Mississippi Delta, are saltwater wetlands that flood from the sea. North America also has huge freshwater wetlands that provide homes and food for many plant and animal species.

Coastal wetlands provide a habitat for many species of birds and other animals. If the character of the wetlands change because of saltwater intrusion, wildlife such as these roseate spoonbills could be destroyed.

Freshwater wetlands would be in danger from two different directions. First, as salt water expands, taking up more room, it moves inland into the freshwater rivers and lakes. The addition of saltwater shocks the plant and animal inhabitants of fresh water. Also, salt water could infiltrate the underground porous rocks, called aquifers, that hold our freshwater drinking supplies.

The second danger to freshwater wetlands is from climate change. It is expected that global warming will bring drought conditions to large parts of the continental interiors, where many wetlands are located. Drought will cause wetlands to dry up, endangering the entire wetland food chain, from snails in the mud to large birds and animals.

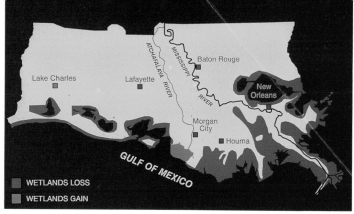

The Louisiana coastline is in continual danger of erosion from the sea. These workers (left) are constructing a wave-dampening fence to lessen the effects of the sea's motion. The map above shows projections of coastal land loss fifty years from now if global warming continues and the sea rises.

Real Estate Loss. In Maine, laws have already been passed decreeing that nothing can be built on the shoreline within the area that scientists predict will disappear as global warming increases.

Not many places are so farsighted. Expensive houses continue to be built within several feet of high water on the ocean coasts. The picture on page 52 shows all that remains of a house lost to coastal erosion. Costly sea-front property is going to disappear unless the people who live there join with everyone else to prevent the global warming.

Biodiversity

When a single plant or animal species disappears from the Earth, its loss often does not seem very important. But we don't know enough about all the food chains that exist on our planet to accurately predict what the long-term effect might be on other species. The plentiful supply of different plant and animal species is called biodiversity. Global warming would harm biodiversity.

We worry about what would happen to people, and yet

Wetland loss could endanger the state bird of Louisiana, the brown pelican. Saltwater intrusion would speed the loss of its nesting grounds.

human beings have the intelligence to predict global warming and can choose to take (or not take) measures to offset it. Other animals and plants have no choice.

Living things do not adjust to rapid change in their living conditions. They die. So if, as many scientists suggest, climate change comes at a pace and in a way we cannot predict, plants, animals, and their ecosystems will suffer. Paleontologists, scientists who study the fossil record of living things, think that the result of rapid global warming will be mass extinctions of many plants and animals.

For example, alligators, which breed in warm, southern climates, have a peculiar way of determining the sex of offspring. Eggs that incubate in a temperature below 93 degrees F. (34 degrees C) turn out to be females. Those that incubate at that temperature or higher turn out to be males. With higher global temperatures, alligators may run out of females, and the species would die out.

An important reason for maintaining biodiversity on our planet is the unknown potential that living plants and animals have. There is no way to know when a particular species of plant or animal may be the answer to an important problem. For example, when the vineyards of France were completely destroyed by a disease, the winemakers of Europe had to come to the United States for wild grape roots that were strong enough to support new growth and a renewed wine industry. If those grape vines, which are pests in the wild, had been destroyed, an entire international industry might have died out.

This kind of potential is one of the prime reasons for preventing loss of plant and animal species. We can't know what will be needed in the future. This is especially true in the tropics, where life-rich rain forest is being destroyed. Well over half of the world's species of plants and animals (estimated at between 10 million and 30 million) are located in tropical regions. Perhaps as many as 50 percent of the medicines prescribed by doctors had their origin in tropical species of plants and animals. If those tropical sources disappeared, fatal diseases that we don't even know about now might go untreated.

A major part of the problem with global warming isn't just that it is happening, but that it is happening so quickly. In the past, it has taken plants and animals thousands of years to adjust to a major change in climate. This time they will not have the opportunity to adjust slowly. It will be a matter of survive the change or die. Since we are already losing—some scientists estimate—150 species of living things *each year*, the loss will be catastrophic.

The rain forests are home to uncountable numbers of plants and animals that have not yet even been identified. Loss of such biodiversity is one of the prices we will pay for allowing global warming.

63

Climate Change

Climate is the normal pattern of weather for an area. "Tropical" and "temperate," for example, are familiar climate zones on our Earth. Scientists predict that the main effect of global warming on climate will be to shift the broad climate belts farther away from the equator.

They think the tropics will extend farther north and south, so that the areas of the southern United States that are now pleasantly warm will become warmer and wetter. One side effect of that change is that the new tropics could also become infested with the disease-carrying insects now found in the present tropics. People in the northern countries have no natural resistance to these diseases and the effects could be devastating.

Scientists also say that the coastal regions of the continents would get more rain than they currently do because of increased evaporation from the oceans. But farther inland, away from the sea, there will probably be less rainfall. This change in moisture, with the increased heat, could have devastating effects on the economies of nations.

Forests. Man might be able to cope with a fast-changing climate, but forests would not. Some trees grow only in certain temperature ranges. If the climate changed slowly, the trees could put out new growth in the newly usable areas at the right pace. But in rapid climate change, the trees might not be able to propagate themselves fast enough. The species could perish. When a species perishes, especially a tree, an entire ecosystem that supports many different living plants and animals could disappear.

In addition to moving farther north—if they can—trees

would also move farther up mountainsides. A species from the foothills might replace the ones that grow higher up. But where would the trees highest up on the mountains go? If the climate change happens too fast, the forests on the mountainsides might die completely, leaving the soil exposed to the elements and erosion.

Studies show that, in general, most eastern American trees such as oaks would spread northward into the Hudson Bay region. That means that the northern conifers would probably disappear. Southern conifers would move north, replacing the oaks. Eastern hemlock and sugar maple might disappear entirely. Western species might be able to move up mountainsides.

Forests can come under stress from any of a variety of causes, such as drought, severe cold—or global warming. A forest already under stress cannot handle another stressful event. It would not be able to fight off an insect infestation, for example, or a wildfire. Forests that are dead or dying could no longer play any role in the carbon dioxide absorption that is one of our main weapons in fighting global warming.

In a rapidly changing climate, forests might not be able to propagate themselves in new territory fast enough for the species to survive.

Agriculture. A British scientist who studied the subject of global warming in the 1930s was enchanted by one aspect which is being studied again: that an increase in carbon dioxide in the atmosphere increases crop yields. He proclaimed that the more carbon dioxide the merrier. When the CO_2 is more concentrated, the plant's stomata—the tiny holes in the leaves—do not have to open as much to allow enough gas to pass into the plant. Thus it loses less water through the stomata, and the plant can grow more quickly.

But botanists have discovered that while crops grow larger and more quickly in a CO_2-strong atmosphere, they also have less protein. They would not provide as good nutrition to animals. Also, animals would have to eat more to get the needed nutrition. Cattle and sheep, however, cannot eat more than they already do because their ruminant stomachs won't digest it any faster than they already do. The total effect would be smaller, less healthy livestock. Additional fertilizers are not the answer because they pollute and add to the cost of food.

The major climate changes that will occur because of global warming are predicted to take place in the temperate zones, where most of the world's people live and where the crops that feed them are grown. Many people think the changes will be beneficial. For example, much of the land of Canada and the Soviet Union, where the growing season has been too short for abundant crops, will develop longer and warmer growing seasons. They could become the grain suppliers to the world. That would happen, though, only if nations have the right kind of soil to support the new crops.

And what will happen to the United States? The major crops in the United

Scientists studying carbon-dioxide use by plants are working to determine the effects global warming might have on our crops.

States have long been hybridized to develop the most abundant harvest with a predictable amount of summer heat and a certain amount of rainfall. If one summer was a little cooler than usual, the crop might be a little smaller. If there was less rainfall than usual, the crops could be irrigated.

Global warming, however, would probably bring a lot more heat and a lot less rain to the central plains of the United States. In 1988, when most of the central states experienced considerable drought, the corn and wheat crops were down almost 40 percent in the Midwest. The soil normally recovers from such a drought; in fact, the rains of 1990 replaced all the missing water in the soil. But under conditions of global warming, there will be no chance to replace the moisture. Every year will be drier, and there will be more and more crop failure. The greatest Wheat Belt in the world could become a desert.

Europe would be luckier than North America or Asia because it is so small that most of its land mass is closer to the sea. It would not suffer the droughtlike conditions that central North America and Asia would experience. But, on the other hand, it might be worse off. There is a possibility, too, that long-term major warming would make the ocean

Canada already produces about one-third as much grain as the United States. It could become the main source of the world's wheat supplies if global warming changes the climate of the Midwest.

Long periods of drought would dry up rivers, leaving behind cracked, unproductive earth (left). Drought leads to famine and starvation when crops can't grow. This woman and child (above) are victims of a drought in Ethiopia.

currents shift, moving the Gulf Stream away from Europe. In consequence, it could become a frozen, glacier-ridden land. The moist rainbelt of Africa might move north, bringing moisture to the deserts of the Sahel, which includes Ethiopia, Chad, and Sudan, where famines are regular occurrences because of drought. That would be good for them, but there is growing evidence that more moisture in the Sahel produces stronger hurricanes in the Atlantic.

The Tundra. One factor that might speed up global warming beyond current predictions is the melting of the tundra. That frozen, barren Arctic land consists of peat (decayed plant matter that, if left alone for millions of years, can turn into coal) held in ice. If the permanently frozen ground, called permafrost, melts, the peat will thaw, releasing huge additional quantities of carbon dioxide and methane.

Man-made structures built on permafrost would also be in danger. The Trans Alaska Pipeline that sends Arctic oil to the lower states is built on permafrost. If the permafrost melts, all structures associated with the pipeline along its 2,000-mile (3,200-kilometer) length would be in danger.

The Great Lakes. Now frozen for more than three months of the year, the Great Lakes shipping waterway would probably be open for eleven months of the year. However, the Midwest would probably be so much drier that the water level might drop as much as 8 feet (2.4 meters). Ships carrying heavy cargoes such as iron ore or grain would not be able to use the lock system to get into Lake Michigan. Harbors would have to be dredged, which might stir up toxic sediments on the bottom, thus poisoning the water.

The Great Lakes have been badly polluted, but they are water sources for bordering states and Canadian provinces. If the lakes shrink, the pollutants will be concentrated into a smaller volume of water. It may be that the Great Lakes as a drinking-water source would come to an end.

All of the "would be's" and "might's" and "probably's" are just that. No one knows absolutely what the effects would be of a major change in the global environment. There is agreement that it won't be all good, that the lives of our children and grandchildren will be changed from what we know now . . . unless we take action now.

An island restaurant in South Carolina (left) was flattened in hours (right) by Hurricane Hugo in 1989. Global warming could contribute to the occurrence of many such devastating storms.

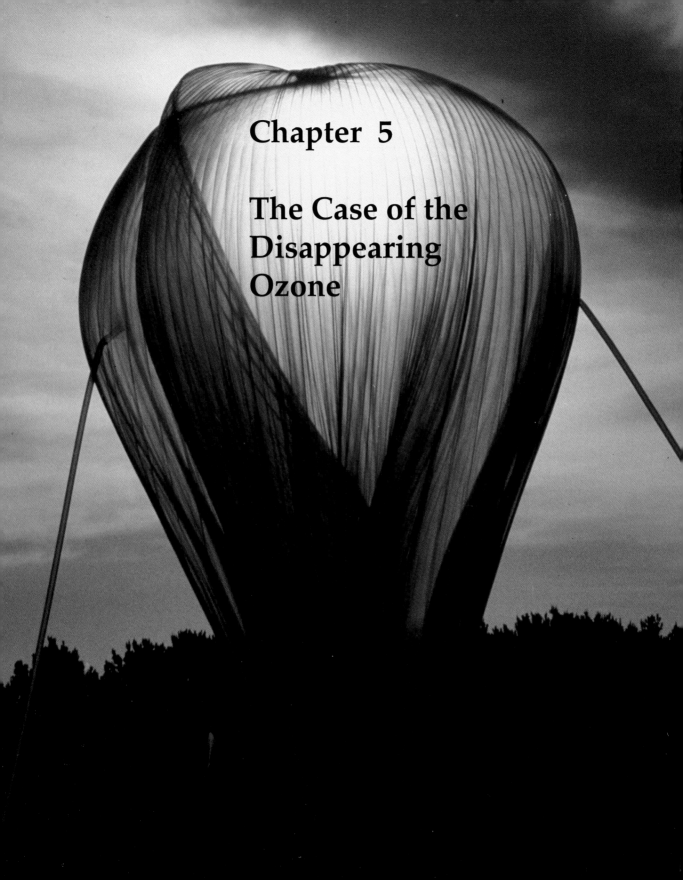

Chapter 5

The Case of the Disappearing Ozone

Ozone is not something that humans make, at least not directly. When sunlight strikes the pollutants making up smog, it breaks oxygen atoms off the polluting chemicals, forming a three-atom molecule of oxygen, called ozone. However, the more pollutants we put into the air, especially through driving gasoline-powered motor vehicles, the more ozone is found in the air.

Ozone in smog is an extraordinarily dangerous pollutant. Within seconds of entering the lungs, ozone has destroyed cell walls. After months of exposure to ozone, the lungs of animals resemble those of heavy smokers. If a single 14-ounce (396-gram) can could be filled with ozone, it could kill 14,000 people. Unfortunately, 80 million Americans live where the air exceeds EPA ozone-pollution standards.

Ozone is also a greenhouse gas that contributes to global warming. But, oddly enough, ozone is not all bad. In the lower atmosphere, the troposphere, it is harmful. But in the upper atmosphere, the stratosphere, it plays a role in climate and it is vital to human and other life.

Molecules of ozone are created when sunlight hits oxygen (O_2) molecules in the upper atmosphere, causing them to split. The loose, single atoms of oxygen quickly join with any molecule that will accept them, usually O_2, which then turns into O_3. These three-atom molecules collect in a thin layer around the globe. This layer, located about 20 miles (32 kilometers) above Earth, is very thin but very important.

Like the three-atom molecules in the troposphere that absorb infrared rays, the three-atom ozone molecules in the stratosphere have the ability to absorb rays from the other end of the solar spectrum—ultraviolet light. The shorter wavelengths of ultraviolet light, called UV-B, can harm humans as well as other animals and plants. Throughout the history of the planet, the ozone layer has been protecting living things on Earth. But now that protective ozone layer is getting thinner.

Ozone Depletion

Normally there is a collection of three different oxygen molecules in the stratosphere. O, O_2, and O_3 have, through ages past, generally been in balance. But strange man-made molecules have been making their way into the stratosphere. Once there, those molecules have changed the molecular balance in the ozone layer so that it is no longer so protective.

What's Happening Up There? In 1973, F. Sherwood Rowland and Mario Molina, chemists at the University of California in Irvine, discovered that some of the chlorofluorocarbons that man had been using since the 1930s rose through the atmosphere into the stratosphere. Once there, the sunlight reacted on them, splitting the chlorine (Cl) atom from the complex CFC molecule. The free Cl reacts with one of the oxygen atoms in ozone (O_3) and pulls it off. That leaves a molecule of regular oxygen (O_2) and a molecule of chlorine monoxide (ClO), neither of which is the least bit of use in protecting Earth from UV-B.

And there is a huge quantity of CFC molecules in the atmosphere. Since Thomas Midgley invented them in 1930, millions of tons have been made and released into the atmosphere. Once there, they don't disappear easily, as most other molecules do. CFCs were developed to be inert—they neither react with other chemicals nor dissolve in water—the

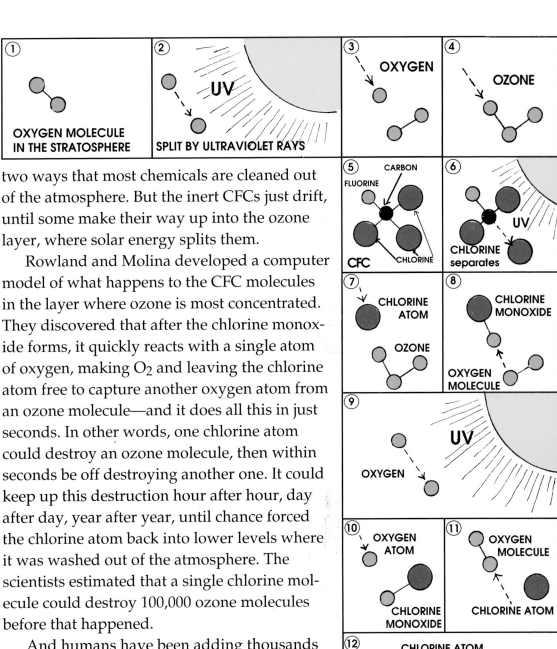

two ways that most chemicals are cleaned out of the atmosphere. But the inert CFCs just drift, until some make their way up into the ozone layer, where solar energy splits them.

Rowland and Molina developed a computer model of what happens to the CFC molecules in the layer where ozone is most concentrated. They discovered that after the chlorine monoxide forms, it quickly reacts with a single atom of oxygen, making O_2 and leaving the chlorine atom free to capture another oxygen atom from an ozone molecule—and it does all this in just seconds. In other words, one chlorine atom could destroy an ozone molecule, then within seconds be off destroying another one. It could keep up this destruction hour after hour, day after day, year after year, until chance forced the chlorine atom back into lower levels where it was washed out of the atmosphere. The scientists estimated that a single chlorine molecule could destroy 100,000 ozone molecules before that happened.

And humans have been adding thousands of tons of CFC molecules to the atmosphere!

Rowland said, "There was no moment when I yelled 'Eureka.' I just came home one night and told my wife, 'The work is going very well, but it looks like the end of the world.'"

What's Happening Down Here? Rowland and Molina announced the results of their work to the world, along with a prediction that at least 7 percent of the ozone layer was going to be destroyed.

But other scientists scoffed at their findings, primarily because they were based on a computer model, and such modeling was fairly new at that time. Also, the chlorine reaction had been studied when the United States was considering building a supersonic transport that had chlorine in the exhaust. That plane was never built, and no one considered that there might be other sources of chlorine—man-made CFCs and related chemicals called halons.

Gradually, the public became concerned, especially since so many people used products containing these CFCs. Perhaps most alarming was the idea that even if we stopped using CFCs right then, they would continue to deplete the ozone for more than 100 years.

Chlorofluorocarbon was originally invented as a refrigerant. Its job in a cooling system is to carry away heat that gets into a refrigerator through the walls and transfer it to the air. CFCs are also used for making the foam-insulation shell that keeps warm air out of the refrigerator in the first place.

FACT

The use of refrigerators is growing worldwide. China, for example, produced only 32,000 refrigerators in 1979, but 4 million in 1987—and there are still hundreds of millions of Chinese families waiting to buy them. They all contain CFCs, although one American company is producing refrigerators that are cooled with helium for the Chinese market.

In addition to being used in making polystyrene plastic foam—called Styrofoam by its maker, Dow Chemical—CFCs became useful as propellants in aerosol cans, such as for deodorants and hairsprays, because they do not react with the product being sprayed. In fact, the companies that made CFCs were taking in about $2 billion a year. They did not want to learn that these products were dangerous to the environment.

By 1976, however, people had begun to be concerned, and sales of aerosols dropped almost in half. The United States, Canada, Sweden, and Norway banned the use of CFCs in aerosol cans. Much of the rest of the world is still using them.

In North America, CFCs in aerosol cans were replaced by several different hydrocarbon gases. These were safer for the upper atmosphere, but were still bad for the lower atmosphere because they added to the ingredients that make smog. At least one company has developed a spray can that uses an expanding piece of plastic that forces the contents of the can out when the button is pushed.

The DuPont Company announced to the world that if science ever positively showed that CFCs were dangerous to the environment, they would stop production. But since

Rowland and Molina's work was based on just a theoretical computer model, they weren't ready to do it.

Nor was that the end of the story. Only a few countries had agreed to the ban, because some additional chemicals were found to be playing a role in ozone depletion, and because aerosol sprays were just one use of CFCs. They were of even more significance in plastic foams and as cleaning agents in the growing electronics industry. When circuits are being cleaned with liquid CFC, the liquid is allowed to evaporate into the air. Oddly enough, electronic circuits can be cleaned just as well with plain old-fashioned soap and water.

The CFC industry's search for substitutes was rather half-hearted, especially because the public appeared to have stopped being concerned—until it was discovered that there was actually a hole in the ozone layer.

The Hole in the Ozone

British scientist Joseph Farman and his colleagues had been taking measurements in the Antarctic each year since the International Geophysical Year in 1957. Then, in the early 1980s, they realized that their ozone measurements over the South Pole had been going down drastically each spring (winter in the Northern Hemisphere) since 1977. They thought their measuring device was faulty and sent it to be repaired. However, the mended one gave even worse answers. This time they published, in 1985, the announcement that there was a hole in the ozone over the South Pole. More than 40 percent of the ozone that should have been in the stratosphere over Antarctica was missing each polar spring.

Those people who wanted to scoff at the measurements were silent when NASA discovered that one of their satel-

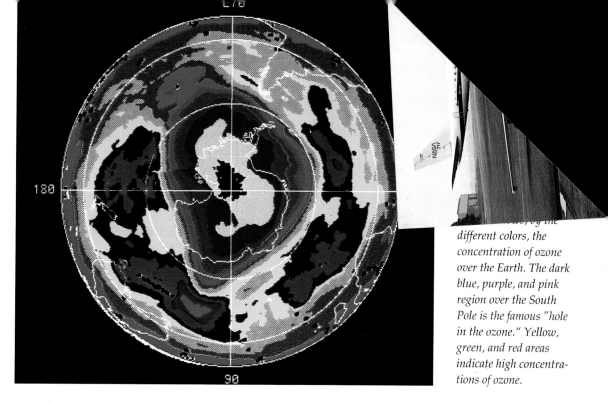

...show, by the different colors, the concentration of ozone over the Earth. The dark blue, purple, and pink region over the South Pole is the famous "hole in the ozone." Yellow, green, and red areas indicate high concentrations of ozone.

lites had obtained similar low readings but the computer had thrown them out because they were absurdly out of line with what was expected.

Soon, numerous scientists descended on Antarctica. The hole was studied from the ground, from balloons, and from a specially equipped airplane that flew into the hole, studying the polar atmosphere's chemistry.

These studies confirmed that the hole develops over the Antarctic each August, at the start of southern spring. It remains stable during October, and then starts to fill in again in November. This is the period when the circular air mass called the polar vortex is strongest. The winds in the stratosphere circulate from the equator toward the poles, so the ozone, newly formed by the sun, concentrates over the poles.

The scientists found that small ice clouds that form in the –130-degree F. (–91-degree C) high-altitude air over the poles are most concentrated during the polar spring because

A DC-8 and a modified U-2 spy plane called the ER-2 (above) were used to carry instruments into the ozone hole above the South Pole. The ER-2 could hold only one person, the pilot, but flew at high altitudes. A pilot, shown below preparing for a test flight, flew a plane that had scientific instruments built into every space possible. The wing pods (below) held equipment to measure various gases. Even the nose held cylinders to scoop up air samples as the aircraft was flown at various altitudes and locations in the Antarctic region.

they form during the winter. The ice crystals may bind up nitrogen, which otherwise is available to interfere with the ozone destruction process. Possibly the ice crystals even speed up ozone destruction.

Since that time, it has been discovered that there is also a hole, but a smaller one, over the Arctic.

One thing scientists have not been able to say is whether

The DC-8 flying laboratory could carry several scientists and their equipment on flights over the South Pole. One scientist (above) measured ozone and polar stratospheric clouds. Another instrument (above right) used laser beams to check the levels of ozone in the atmosphere above the plane's flight path.

Other methods of studying ozone are carried out elsewhere. This balloon (right) carries an instrument to an altitude of 24 miles (39 kilometers) above Texas to measure the presence of the molecules that break down ozone. Such tests over the United States reveal that the ozone layer is disappearing over populated areas.

polar holes exist because of the strange structure of the polar atmosphere or whether they are the forerunner of a serious and sudden depletion of the whole ozone layer. However, scientists meeting together in 1988 decreed: "Without chlorofluorocarbons, there would be no hole in the ozone."

The World Reacts. Now even industry became seriously concerned. McDonald's was one of the world's largest users

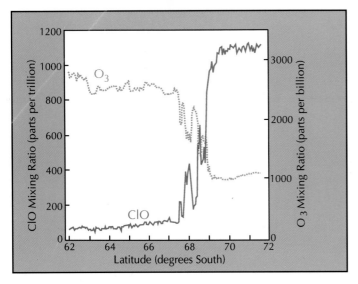

NASA's ER-2 research plane flew into the polar vortex over Antarctica, and instruments graphed the change in abundance of ozone (O_3) and chlorine monoxide (ClO). It shows that as the plane reaches 69 degrees south latitude, chlorine overwhelms the ozone, making the "hole in the ozone."

of polystyrene foam in the boxes it used for its Big Macs and other sandwiches. It reacted immediately by banning the use of CFCs in the polystyrene foam it buys for use in the United States. The DuPont Company began to make good on its promise of ten years before. In one year alone, the major producer of CFCs spent $70 million on the search for safe replacements.

The most promising answer is the production of substances that do the same job as Freon and other CFCs but break down more quickly when they enter the atmosphere. The secret is in putting hydrogen into the CFC formula, because then it reacts at lower levels and the molecules won't last long enough to reach the ozone layer. For example, CFC-11, which is used to make foam for furniture, can be replaced with CFC-123, or methylene chloride. The latter is suspected of being carcinogenic, or cancer-causing. Pentane is a hydrocarbon that can be used in expanding polystyrene into foam, but it is quite flammable, so the manufacturing process is more dangerous. Such hydrogen-bearing formulas are often called HFCs or HCFCs.

After a meeting in 1987, 34 nations agreed in the Montreal Protocol to reduce CFC emissions by 50 percent by the year 2000. Two years later, 80 nations meeting at Helsinki, Finland, agreed to ban all CFCs. However, there were no penalties for failure to comply with the Protocol and the cutback in production was based on population, which continues to increase. In addition, the United States was not among the signers, although it has slowed CFC use by putting a tax of $1.37 on each pound (448 grams) of CFCs used.

Individual states are beginning to take some action. Vermont, for example, has banned the use of CFC-12 in automobile air conditioners built from 1993 on. In the summer of 1990, Irvine, California, became perhaps the first city in the United States to outlaw the buying, selling, or use of CFCs. All car-repair stations that deal in air conditioners have to install Freon-capturing systems. They are delighted to discover that they save money.

Most cars have air conditioners powerful enough to cool a whole medium-sized house, in order to cool off the car quickly after it has been parked in the sunshine. When the outside air is above 100 degrees F. (38 degrees C), the inside of a car parked in sun can become hotter than the boiling point of water, 212 degrees F. (100 degrees C). Car air conditioners make up the largest single use of CFCs.

FACT

In 1988 the use of CFCs worldwide broke down as follows, in millions of pounds (kilograms): as refrigerants, 750 (337); as foaming agents, 730 (328); in aerosols, 480 (216); as

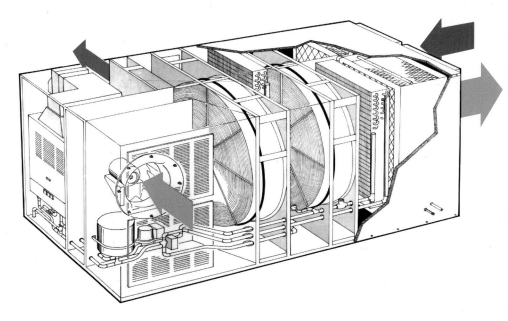

Air-conditioning systems that do not use CFCs to transfer heat from the inside to the outside air have already been developed. The system shown here both heats and cools a building with rotating wheels containing dessicants, which are absorbent materials that draw moisture from the air.

Outside air goes in at the lower arrow, is dried, and sent into the building at the far end. Inside air enters at the far end and is exhausted out the top left.

cleansers, 480 (216); in all other uses, 100 (45). Carbon tetra-chloride, a chemical that used to be important in the laundry industry, and methyl chloroform, an industrial solvent, have also been found to add chlorine to the ozone layer. They are being phased out of industrial use.

The hole did not grow as large as expected in 1988, probably because of the strange weather phenomena over the entire globe. However, in 1990, the hole was even bigger.

That same year, in November, industrial nations meeting at Geneva, Switzerland, proposed a plan to pay developing Third World nations to refrain from using CFCs and to use ozone-friendly chemicals (which cost more) instead. The plan was directed primarily at China and India, which have refused to cut back on CFC use. They are trying to raise the standard of living in their countries by major increases in the use of refrigeration, one of the prime uses of CFCs. Again, the United States government failed to agree with the plan.

Rowland told *Popular Science* magazine, "Even if we act now, we can expect to see the worst stages of ozone depletion around the year 2020."

UV-B Damage to People

The hole in the ozone over the Arctic region, while not as severe as the one over the Antarctic, is more important to people because it stretches down across the most heavily populated regions of the Earth. Over the city of Moscow, for example, there is 20 percent less ozone protecting the people during winter than there is the rest of the year.

So what? you may wonder. Why all the fuss?

Each 1 percent drop in ozone is thought to allow a 2 to 3 percent rise in ultraviolet light reaching the Earth. Each drop of 1 percent in ozone allows 2 percent more UV-B to reach us, increasing skin cancer by 3 to 6 percent. Already, more than half a million cases of skin cancer are reported each year in the United States alone.

Skin Cancer. Cancer is a disease in which some cells in the body go out of control. They start growing strangely, and eventually in huge numbers, harming the healthier parts of the body. Skin cancer always starts on the parts of the body that are exposed directly to too much sun. The simple kind of skin cancer, called carcinoma, can usually be cured if caught early by removal of the problem cells. It can be recognized from any red scaly spot or small open sore that does not heal. Although rarely fatal, this cancer can destroy cells deep into the skin.

The more dangerous type of skin cancer, called malignant melanoma, starts in the pigment-forming cells of the skin and readily spreads, or metastasizes, to other parts of the body. UV-B is known to play a role in the development of melanoma, but its direct link is not known. The incidence of melanoma in the United States exactly doubled during the

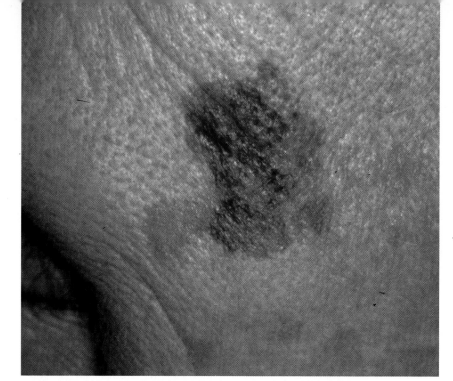

This melanoma on a woman's cheek marks the beginning of serious skin cancer caused by sun damage to the skin.

1980s. Melanoma can be caught early by keeping an eye out for any change in a mole that you already have.

One in every 150 North Americans will get skin cancer at some time in their lives. Caucasians are affected 10 times more often than blacks, and the closer white-skinned people live to the equator (where the sun's rays are more direct), the more likely they are to get skin cancer. Interestingly, the incidence of melanoma on blacks' non-pigmented skin (the palms of the hands and the soles of the feet) is identical to those areas in whites. The sexes differ somewhat in terms of where skin cancer occurs. Men frequently develop tumors on the tips of ears and scalp, due to the balding process. Women get more cancers on the lower legs, which are exposed to sunlight when wearing skirts and dresses.

One direct proof of the involvement of the sun in skin cancer is the fact that in North America, where drivers sit on the left side of the car, more cancer occurs on their left sides. In Great Britain, where drivers sit on the right, skin cancer happens most often on the drivers' right sides. Australians, who are light-skinned and live within the spreading ozone hole, have the highest rate of skin cancer in the world.

In North America, an individual's lifetime risk for melanoma has soared by 1000 percent since the 1930s, primarily because sunbathing has become so popular. In fact, there has been a 30 percent increase just since 1978 in the chance of developing cancer.

What can you do? Melanoma appears to occur in people who were severely sunburned, usually in childhood. The simpler skin cancers are related to continuous exposure to the sun. Ultraviolet from the sun is at its height at midday. Stay away from the beaches between 10 and 2. Always wear sun screen with a protection number of at least 15, and be sure to reapply it after swimming.

The International Trans-Antarctic Expedition, led by Will Steger, crossed the polar continent by dogsled in the polar summer of 1989-90, during the appearance of the hole in the ozone. The team had to wear specially made clothing that prevented UV-B from reaching their skin.

Not just humans are subject to sunburn from ultraviolet. Cows, for example, might have to graze after dark if the ozone depletion continues.

Cataracts. Prolonged exposure to ultraviolet radiation is also known to cause cataracts, which is a fogging of the lens of the eye that dims one's eyesight. Cataracts frequently form during old age, but they are now occurring earlier in response to the depleted ozone layer.

For those people who can afford it, surgery can be used to repair cataracts. Worldwide, however, this disease blinds

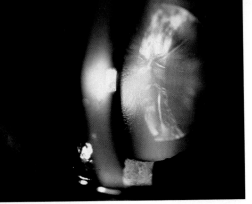

The clouding of the eye called cataracts will blind an increasing number of people if the ozone layer continues to be depleted.

12 million to 15 million people and seriously impairs the vision of another 18 million to 30 million. The increasing number of cases can be lowered only by repairing the ozone layer.

Immune System. The built-in mechanism with which our bodies fight disease is called our immune system. Without it, we would be seriously ill from common colds, catch every disease bug that was in the air, and probably not last very long. Scientists have discovered that UV-B damages those cells that fight infections. It may even trigger the actions of other cells that suppress immune functions.

In the case of damage to our immune systems, wearing sunscreen lotions when we swim is not enough. The only thing that will help prevent such damage is to stay indoors or, even better, to act now to repair the ozone layer.

Other Damage from Ultraviolet

Scientists analyzing twenty years of data have found that the ozone layer over the mid-Northern Hemisphere, where our major food crops grow, has thinned by almost 3 percent. Botanists who tested more than 300 crop plants in increased levels of ultraviolet found that the quality and growth of about two-thirds of them were seriously affected. Some of our basic vegetable crops fail to produce the way they should under too much UV. Combined with crop damage from global warming, the increase in ultraviolet light could seriously harm the food supplies of our planet.

Harm in the Sea. Of course it's not only the land that receives UV-B radiation. Over 70 percent of the Earth's surface is made up of ocean. The UV-B rays strike deeply into the water, penetrating as much as 65 feet (20 meters). Again it's the basic cell structure of the living things that can be harmed, especially cells of tiny, vulnerable sea creatures.

The base of the ocean food chain is microscopic plant life called phytoplankton. Phytoplankton has the ability to photosynthesize—to convert sunlight and carbon dioxide into food and energy. It then serves as the food for tiny crustaceans called krill, which are eaten by bigger creatures, and so on up the food chain. The fish that humans depend on thrive because of phytoplankton. However, UV-B harms the tiny plants' ability to photosynthesize food, and the entire ocean food chain is weakened.

UV-B that strikes the water around coral reefs can harm larger creatures. A number of the animals that make up those beautiful and fragile places are killed by direct exposure to UV-B. Others fail to reproduce properly. Coral reefs have been endangered by a number of environmental problems, such as pollution. The longer they are exposed to abnormal ultraviolet light because of the weakened ozone layer, the greater are the chances that coral reefs are doomed to be a thing of the past.

Phytoplankton, shown here greatly magnified, are microscopic plants at the base of the ocean food chain. They can be damaged by ultraviolet rays that pass through the depleted ozone layer and reach into the ocean, thus endangering all sea life.

The Ozone Layer and the Greenhouse Effect

At first glance, the ozone layer depletion going on far up in the stratosphere and the global warming going on down in the troposphere appear to be two unrelated problems. But remember what we said about forests. Living things that are already under stress cannot withstand rapid change from another stressful event. In other words, if living things on

ENJOY YOUR HOT CHOCOLATE!

Curtis A. Moore, writing in *International Wildlife* magazine, described how one plastic-foam cup, such as you might drink hot chocolate from and then throw away, can contribute to the destruction of our planet.

Step 1. The cup is made of billions of tiny bubbles made firm by one billion billion molecules of CFCs. Each molecule has the ability to last up to 150 years before it disintegrates. The gases enter the air when the cup is smashed or burned.

Step 2. The gases in the atmosphere, along with other greenhouse gases, trap heat, helping to raise the average global temperature. The molecules remain in the atmosphere up to fifteen years before they gradually break free and drift up into the stratosphere.

Step 3. Twenty-five miles (40 kilometers) above the Earth, the CFC molecules enter the ozone layer. There they are broken apart by the ultraviolet radiation from the sun and individual chlorine atoms are released. Each one, during its 150-year lifetime, can destroy 100,000 ozone atoms by joining up, temporarily, with one of the oxygen atoms. The two remaining oxygen atoms are made up of regular breathable oxygen, which doesn't do a thing to stop ultraviolet radiation. Gradually the ozone layer is weakened. Ultraviolet radiation then

Earth have to adjust to more ultraviolet radiation, they won't have the strength to handle global warming.

There is evidence that increased UV-B striking pollution in the lower atmosphere will increase the amount of ozone in the air. Ozone, of course, is one of the main constituents of smog and also a greenhouse gas. So if the protective ozone layer is weakened, global warming is increased.

reaches the ocean, where microscopic plants and animals—the base of the food chain—are destroyed.

Step 4. Smog levels rise, destroying forests. Along with the loss of habitat go many plant and animal species.

Step 5. Tropospheric ozone, along with the other greenhouse gases, warms the atmosphere enough to melt the tundra in the Arctic.

Step 6. The melting of the top levels of the tundra releases methane and other gases, which increase the level of greenhouse gases in an unstoppable cycle of more melting and more methane.

Step 7. Methane (CH_4) rises through the atmosphere into the stratosphere, where it reacts with ozone (O_3) to form water (H_2). The water crystallizes into ice clouds, which facilitate the ozone depletion.

Step 8. The warming of the Earth's surface warms the oceans. At first there is a great abundance of life in the warmer seas, but because the ozone depletion is allowing ultraviolet rays to destroy the food chain, this new abundance cannot survive on the available nutrients.

Step 9. No one really knows for sure what happens next. Anything might happen, but it is certain that Earth would be nothing like the world we know today.

Chapter 6

The Solution:
Changing the
Way We Live

It's hard to realize that what the world might be like fifty years from now is as important for us to think about today as our next science exam or earning a living. We can ignore the problem of global warming and hope that the climate modelers are wrong. But if they are right, the problems could become overwhelming before any effort is made to stop them.

Fortunately, if we tackle most air-pollution problems, we also tackle the global warming problem. For example, ozone forms in the air when sunlight hits nitrogen oxides and hydrocarbons that are emitted by cars and smokestacks. That ozone is gradually spreading out even into rural areas where it is endangering trees. We need all the trees we can get to help remove carbon from the air. Forests are also being killed by acid rain, which is caused by sulfur from coal being turned to acid when it hits water vapor.

Turning Off the Oil

We know we can cut fossil-fuel use. From 1973 to 1986, the American economy grew by one-third, without increasing the consumption of energy at all. These were the years when imported oil costs were kept very high. Many people stopped driving "gas guzzlers," and bought smaller, fuel-efficient cars. The government gave special tax credits to companies working on developing alternative energy sources, which might one day free us from dependence on foreign oil.

Then the Organization of Petroleum Exporting Countries (OPEC) lost its unity. Some of the member countries—all of whom had agreed to keep oil prices high—reduced their prices and raised their production. When plenty of oil was

One gallon (3.8 liters) of gasoline puts about 20 pounds (9 kilograms) of carbon dioxide into the atmosphere. A "gas guzzler" getting 12 miles per gallon (5 kilometers per liter) emits two or even three times more CO_2 than a fuel-efficient car.

available on the market (in part because people had been conserving energy so well), the government no longer saw a reason to keep investing in renewable energy sources. Research and development in those areas stopped. Big cars became popular again.

Then, in 1990, Iraq invaded Kuwait for its petroleum, and the price of oil rose abruptly. People talked about alternative energy for a while. Then the price of oil went down again.

It will take a public, national decision to stop depending on oil—our own oil as well as oil from other countries—and help the environment and our economy by building power supplies using fuels that don't contribute to global warming.

The major areas in which we can take action to solve the problem of global warming are: 1) cutting back on carbon dioxide emissions, 2) developing renewable forms of energy, and 3) reforesting the globe.

Limiting Fossil-Fuel Use

Even to slow the increase in CO_2 to about one-third of the rate at which it is currently increasing (about 0.6 percent annually), we would need to cut our use of coal and other fossil fuels by 60 percent.

The wonderful thing about cutting down on fossil fuel use in order to help repair the greenhouse effect is that such conservation has marvelous side benefits. Acid rain will be checked, natural resources conserved, pollution eased.

Since the Industrial Revolution started we have never cut back, but now is the time to start.

Efficient Cars. If your family's car gets approximately 22 miles per gallon (9.3 kilometers per liter), it gives off 0.9 pound (0.4 kilogram) of CO_2 for every mile it is driven. If you miss your school bus and have to be driven 2 miles (3.2 kilometers) to school (and the car returns the same distance), your trip is putting 3.6 pounds (1.6 kilograms) of carbon dioxide into the air—just for you to get to school. Your bus would have put more CO_2 into the air, but it would be transporting perhaps 20 or 30 students.

A car that gets only 18 miles per gallon (7.6 kilometers per liter), which was the average for cars driving American roads in 1988, will produce more than 57 tons (51 metric tons) of carbon dioxide during its lifetime. A car that gets 26.5 miles per gallon (11.2 kilometers per liter), the standard set for 1989 cars, will emit 20 tons (18 metric tons) less.

New cars should be made of lightweight materials and have smaller engines. They should be aerodynamically styled (streamlined) to eliminate wind resistance, which requires the engine to use more fuel to overcome it. In 1990, some little cars got three times the gas mileage of average cars, so we know it can be done.

The major car companies already have the ability to build cars that get

This chemist is working on testing gasohol, a combination of gasoline and ethanol, which is alcohol made from corn and other vegetables. The alcohol content cuts down on the CO_2 going into the atmosphere.

100 miles to the gallon (42 kilometers per liter), but they will not retool their factories to build them until the government or the general public demands such cars.

States cannot order car changes, but in 1990 the northeastern states followed a different approach. They agreed to help reduce global warming by changing the gasoline used in those states. It will be less volatile—turn to gas less easily—so that there is less CO_2 in the emissions.

In Canada and elsewhere, some drivers are having their cars fixed to handle natural gas. It burns cleaner than gasoline, and is available all over the world. The disadvantages are that the car cannot accelerate as well, the gas tank is bulkier, and it has to be filled more often.

Even more to the point, however, will be the building and using of major mass-transit systems. People need to see an advantage to themselves in using buses, trains, subways, and airplanes, especially suburbanites who travel into a city each day. The most obvious benefit would be the chance to save money. That means convenient new systems, tax support for the systems so that fares are reasonable, and high taxes on cars and gasoline.

Buildings. About one-third of our energy resources are used for heating and cooling buildings. That amount could

Cars of the future may run on electricity. This van (below) plugs into an electric outlet at night to recharge its batteries. Solar cars are fueled by sunlight striking solar cells that make electricity. The one shown at the right was designed by engineering students in 1990 for a national solar-car race.

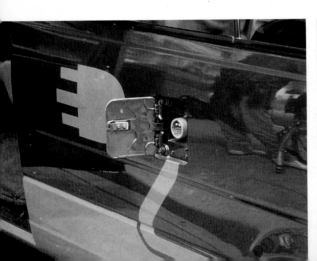

be cut just by making certain that all buildings are leak-free when they are built, and kept in good repair thereafter.

They can also be built with better insulation. Recently, most insulation has been CFC-expanded rigid foam. Finding a better and different insulation would help solve two problems—depletion of the ozone layer and heat leakage.

Considerable research is going into insulation for refrigerators, which has generally used CFC-made foam. About 7 percent of all power used goes for refrigeration. About one-third of that amount could be eliminated if new refrigerators and freezers had walls built like vacuum, or Thermos, bottles—having double layers of glass or another strong material with the air between them removed. Heat moves poorly through a vacuum, so warm air doesn't get in.

With more and more skyscrapers reaching into the cold winds of the skies, heat loss through windows is important. Work is being done to develop windows that have an insulating gel between the two layers. They will be much more effective than regular double-paned windows, which just have air between the layers of glass.

It's important for the halting of global warming that people use mass transportation systems, such as subways, whenever possible. Cars usually carry only one or two people, but many people are transported in trains and subways for the amount of emissions given off.

An electricity-generating plant near the Grand Canyon burns huge quantities of coal. Some of the smog created by the emissions is settling in the canyon.

Power Plants. Over half of the fossil fuel burned goes to generate electric power, so whatever we can do to cut emissions from power plants is helpful. That percentage will rise as power is brought to more "have-not" countries. Third World nations working to improve their standard of living are reluctant to consider limiting their use of energy before they even really get started.

Power plants normally depend on coal, a mineral that is available all over the world in huge quantities. But there are different grades of coal, with different quantities of polluting impurities in them. It may be necessary for governments of industrialized countries to pay producers of "bad" coal to switch to coal that burns cleaner. The polluting coal can just be left in the ground.

Another method being used is to build power plants next to major manufacturing plants so that the heat used in manufacturing is not wasted but is used to create electric power. This process is called cogeneration. The problem is that cogeneration requires regional planning. Someone has to know that one town wants to build a power plant and perhaps a company is planning a factory, and that individual has to have the authority to bring the two groups together for everyone's benefit.

Alternative Energy

In an electric-generating plant, a fuel is usually needed to boil water. The steam given off by the boiling water is funneled so that it strikes flat blades of a device called a turbine. The rotating of the turbine moves a wire coil through a magnetic field. As it moves, the magnetic field changes, becoming electricity. But the point is—it doesn't matter to the electricity being generated what creates the initial heat that makes steam.

Coal has been used to boil the water for over one hundred years. Oil has been used for a shorter period. Recently, trash has been used as a form of keeping waste out of landfills. Chopped-up tires can be used, as can the methane given off by decomposing garbage in landfills. All these methods put more carbon dioxide into the air but less than would be released from coal or oil.

We need heat sources that do not spew CO_2 into the atmosphere or use up natural resources. These alternative forms are called renewable energy sources. There are basically six of them: nuclear energy, hydropower, geothermal energy, wind energy, solar energy, and biomass energy.

Nuclear Energy. The easiest change we can make is to use nuclear energy for power generation. When the nucleus of an atom is split apart, it gives off huge quantities of energy. This is called fission. Unfortunately, the environmentalists who have fought so hard to solve global warming have also fought against the use of nuclear energy. If that is not an acceptable answer, most of our answers must come from the development of alternative energy sources.

No new nuclear power plant has been ordered in the United States since 1978. Nuclear power plants are hugely expensive to build—costing at least twice as much as a coal-fired plant. Also, if something goes wrong with nuclear materials, they can send deadly radiation into the atmosphere. When the reactor at Chernobyl in the Soviet Union exploded in 1986, about 30 people died immediately, hundreds were burned, and thousands more were exposed to radiation and can expect to suffer from radiation-caused cancer at some time in their lives. Entire towns had to be permanently abandoned. After the disaster at Chernobyl, people fought against nuclear power even more firmly.

Because nuclear power generation does not produce greenhouse gases, however, there has been considerable talk of returning to the full development of nuclear power plants. Many physicists think that safer, smaller, and cheaper plants can be built than were constructed in the past. However, there are unsolved problems of what to do with nuclear waste, how to keep the environment safe from radiation, and how to keep nuclear fuel out of the hands of governments who might turn it into nuclear bombs.

Fusion is another way of producing energy from atoms. Instead of fission, which splits the nucleus, fusion joins two nuclei. Hydrogen is turned into helium. This process has been achieved at exceedingly high temperatures, but cooler —and therefore cheaper—methods of fusion have not yet been accomplished beyond the laboratory. Fusion is a good possibility for the future, however.

Hydropower. Hydropower is water power, the power of dams and waterfalls. When water falls a distance, its energy can be used to turn the turbine of a generator. Already, about 10 percent of America's electrical needs are met by hydropower. Also, it is estimated that perhaps 50 percent of those locations where hydroelectric dams could be built have already been constructed, and there are environmental reasons why some of the remaining sites should not be used. Large dams can harm a river. So hydroelectric power cannot grow much, but it is cheaper than any other form of energy.

Another form of water power called thermal storage technology uses huge water-storage tanks that cool during the night. The next day, the water is distributed through the building to air-condition it.

This dam in the Bonneville Power Administration contributes hydropower to a system that supplies electricity to almost half of the American Northwest.

Hot steam pours from the ground after a test hole has been drilled. The steam can be used to turn turbines for generating electricity.

Geothermal energy. Geothermal energy is heat stored within the Earth. It can be used in several different ways. Hydrothermal energy comes from steam released from the ground. Iceland, for example, has many places where steam spouts from the ground. The heat is used directly to produce steam for turning turbines.

Magma, the hot, molten rock of volcanoes, could also be used to generate electricity. Pipes can be driven into the ground and heat carried through them to water tanks.

In some places, such as north of San Francisco, California, heated air under high pressure (called dry steam) rushes from the earth. It can be used directly to turn turbines. Other sources on the East Coast are not hot enough to produce steam, but they could at least be used to heat buildings.

Geothermal energy is not really renewable, but the only limit on its quantity is the limit of the heat within the Earth itself. Most geothermal sources give off only a tiny fraction of carbon dioxide compared to coal.

Wind Energy. The wind is free. Using wind to turn the turbines that produce electricity makes no impact on the environment. Farmers worldwide have used windmills for thousands of years to grind corn and pump water. Starting in the 1920s, farms across America moved into the modern age using electricity generated by windmills. Now windmills are being used to contribute to big power networks.

A windmill "farm" at Altamont Pass, California, has 7,000 windmills producing electric power. The power is sold to the local power company, which feeds it into its normal

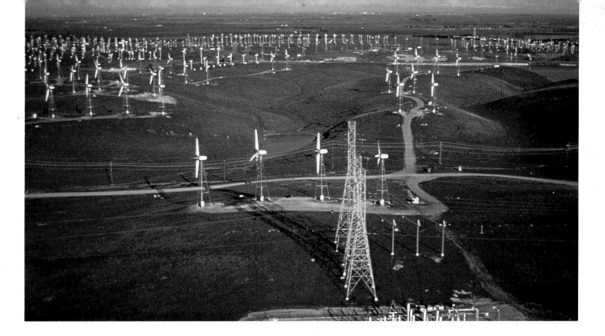

system. By 1987, the state of California had more wind-power generation than any other place in the world—17,000 machines generating 1500 kilowatts of electricity.

A big wind-generating system would take up hundreds or even thousands of square miles in total. But each windmill, or wind turbine, needs little land, so the system could be spread out across suburbs or even cities. Also, windmills can be built on scrub land that has no other usefulness.

Solar Energy. Both wind and hydroelectric power can be counted as solar energy because they ultimately come from the sun. But here we'll deal with those methods that directly use the sun's rays.

Each year, enough sunlight falls on Earth to meet the United States' energy needs for 500 years. Sunlight can be used to produce both heat and electricity, so it is usable for just about any energy use except mass transportation.

There are two ways of using solar energy. Solar thermal energy is the heating power of sunlight. The sun's rays strike mirrors that concentrate the heat on water or oil in tanks or

Altamont Pass in California is the site of one of the largest windmill "farms" in the world. Each wind turbine can feed 100 kilowatts of electricity into the local power grid.

Solar energy is already being used in a variety of ways.

Above, *a batteryless pumping system provides water in Mali, Africa.*
Top right, *a small, portable solar panel powers an electric trolling motor for fishing.*
Right, *a similar small panel can be used to power a portable computer so that no batteries are necessary.*
Below, *a photovoltaic array built into the roof of a house provides electricity.*
Below right, *a solar-energy research and manufacturing facility requires huge arrays of photovoltaic cells that generate almost thirty times as much electricity as those on the house.*

pipes. The liquid heats and is then piped through the house where it provides heat or warms water. It can also be used to boil water to produce electricity. The cost of solar thermal power is nearing the cost of coal-fired electricity.

Photovoltaic energy is electricity produced directly by light rays acting on semiconductors, special negatively charged materials that react to the photons (positive charges) in sunlight to produce electricity. Solar cells are small photovoltaic (light-electricity) devices that were first used on satellites where moving parts could not be used. They are very useful on Earth to provide power for calculators and other such small devices, but they are not yet economical for use in a power system. However, research is being done to make the production of photovoltaics cheaper and easier.

One scientist has figured out that all the power used in the United States could be generated by 4,000 square miles (10,400 square kilometers) of solar cells spread out on any flat, sunny surface. The problem is storing it.

Solar power might also be used to split liquid water (H_2O) into the two gases that make it up—hydrogen and oxygen. The hydrogen—a very clean fuel—could be piped into furnaces and burned to produce heat and electric power or used to run the engines of modified cars.

Biomass. Biomass energy is energy derived from wood and other vegetation. The vegetation is not used directly for burning—that would just put all that carbon back into the atmosphere. Instead, it is treated to make clean-burning fuel. Gasohol, for example, is a mixture of regular gasoline and ethanol, an alcohol derived from corn or grain. It burns well in cars and cuts carbon emissions by about 8 percent.

An Earth Experience

How Trees Take in CO₂

Green plants carry on photosynthesis, the making of sugar from carbon dioxide and water in the presence of sunlight. A tree with thousands of leaves needs a tremendous amount of carbon dioxide, much more than any other green plant, to keep all the billions of cells in all parts of the tree alive and functioning.

You can demonstrate how leaves get CO_2 into their chloroplasts in order to manufacture food for the enormous trunks, branches, and roots—carbon that is released when a tree decomposes or is burned.

Select a tree in your backyard or a nearby park where you can reach three leaves on one branch. Make a label with the word TOP and tie it to the stem of a leaf. Attach the word BOTTOM to a second leaf and label the third BOTH SIDES.

Spread a coating of clear petroleum jelly or other thick, greasy material on the top of the first leaf, the bottom of the second, and both sides of the third. Be sure that the entire surface is covered and that you put the grease only on the designated surfaces.

Observe the leaves daily. It may take two weeks before a noticeable change occurs. What conclusions can you draw?

Most trees in a deciduous forest have the majority of the pores, or stomata, on the underside of the leaves. During daylight, when photosynthesis is carried on, these pores open up. They permit both the entrance of carbon dioxide and the exit of water.

You can deduce the enormous amount of CO_2 that just one tree takes in during one day. Imagine the quantity consumed by millions of acres of trees.

Biomass is, of course, completely renewable. In fact, it would be simple to have energy plantations devoted strictly to growing usable vegetation that would be replanted each time it was cut. That method may seem to just balance out the carbon. But actually, new-growing trees take in more carbon than is released by burning old trees, so there would be an overall improvement in the CO_2 balance. A great deal of municipal waste—mixed paper, food scraps, garden waste, and plastics—could also be used for biomass energy.

A poplar seedling is being measured to check its growth in a controlled environment. Such research is directed toward developing plant farms that would grow trees for use as biomass fuel.

Renewable energy will not be able to compete unless the price we pay for fossil fuels is raised to include a cost for environmental damage, such as air pollution and acid rain. A Natural Resources Defense Council study reported that electricity made from coal-burning and nuclear-energy plants should have an added cost of at least 2 to 3 cents per kilowatt-hour. Government subsidies also add to the cost, bringing it well above the cost of alternative sources.

"Plant a Tree, Cool the Globe"

Third World countries want to progress economically as other nations have done. Most of them need to do this in order to pay off their huge debts to industrialized countries. Cutting down forests to make cattle ranches and burning wood for power generation help do that. But industrialized countries, knowing that deforestation promotes global warming, are opposed. Deforestation contributes about 20 percent to global warming.

these debts or even pay poorer nations not to cut the forests. Since we will have to pay huge sums of money to make corrections in the atmosphere anyway, we might as well sacrifice repayment of the loans to keep the excess CO_2 out of the atmosphere in the first place.

Brazil, for example, has said that it will be willing to replace the trees it cuts and to reduce cutting—if it is paid enough for the wood products to justify the reduced cutting. This idea has been called "Debt-for-Nature." In 1990 the United Nations called for a "Law of the Atmosphere," which would raise taxes on fossil fuel. These taxes would be used to pay other nations to reduce deforestation.

Of course, it's not just forests somewhere far away that are a problem. Most of North America was forested when settlers came. Most of those forests have disappeared, but now we need trees to help solve global warming.

The Miracle Tree. A fast-growing tree captures and holds about 48 pounds (22 kilograms) of carbon dioxide each year. All kinds of trees absorb CO_2 at about the same rate—if they receive equal amounts of sunlight and water. During winter or drought, little CO_2 is used because the trees are dormant. Therefore, tropical trees are better than northern trees at absorbing CO_2. Also, the older the forest, the less carbon dioxide is absorbed, but old trees hold huge amounts of it.

One utility that is building a 1,000-megawatt, coal-fired power plant in New England decided to balance emissions by planting trees. They will plant a forest of 52 million trees in rural Guatemala over the next ten years.

The timber industry suggests that we should cut down old trees and replace them with new ones because young,

One acre (0.4 hectare) of trees absorbs about 10 tons (9 metric tons) of carbon dioxide each year. Researchers have found that an old forest of 450-year-old Douglas fir trees, such as those in the photograph, holds more than twice as much carbon as a forest less than 200 years old would hold.

growing trees absorb more CO_2 than old ones do. Also, if old trees were cut for lumber, the carbon in them would be locked up instead of re-leased by decomposition. But old forests hold more carbon than new, so the plan would not help.

Resources for the Future, a Washington, D.C. organization, has suggested that we could soak up all the 2.9 billion tons (2.6 billion metric tons) of CO_2 that goes into the atmosphere each year by planting 1.1 billion acres (0.4 billion hectares) of new forest—the size of all the states west of the Mississippi, minus Alaska and Hawaii.

To try to reverse the concentration of CO_2 to levels the world knew one hundred years ago would require a forest an impossible 124,000 square miles (320,000 square kilometers) in size. While it was growing, it would soak up a billion tons (0.9 billion metric tons) of carbon dioxide each year. And it would still take 152 years to revert to old CO_2 levels.

Big Users of Carbon Dioxide

For this experiment you will need at least two or three different kinds of locations. You might select a home or school yard with numerous trees on the grounds. Find a place in town where there is only concrete and buildings but little traffic. An in-between type of test site could be a grassland community, such as an open field.

Prepare three shallow glass dishes of limewater (see page 20 for instructions). At each site, set one dish where it will not be disturbed for a period of three hours.

Collect the dishes and examine them closely. When carbon dioxide from the air mixes with the limewater, a thin white crust forms on the dish, indicating the presence of this colorless gas. Use a magnifying glass to see which sample has the thickest crust.

The Other Miracle. Trees not only absorb carbon dioxide, they also provide shade and coolness, thus cutting down on the need for power. Trees planted to shield a house can prevent great quantities of CO_2 from going into the atmosphere each year. Three well-placed trees around a house can cut air-conditioning needs for that house by 10 to 15 percent.

The American Forestry Association started Global ReLeaf, a campaign to expand new forests, reduce deforestation, and help reduce dependence on fossil fuels. Their immediate goal is to plant 100 million healthy trees around homes and businesses in cities and towns by 1992. That number of trees could save $4 billion a year in air-conditioning bills. We save money as individuals, the trees absorb carbon dioxide, and fossil fuel is not burned.

International Agreement

The Dutch minister of the environment said in a 1989 speech at the White House: "We needed Love Canal before hazardous waste was tackled. We needed a dying River Rhine before waste waters were treated. We needed forest dieback in Central Europe before acid rain was recognized as an urgent problem. My country has decided to learn the lessons from the past and act on global warming now."

Each country must do the same, and all countries must act together. Global warming is really the first completely international problem that the world has ever faced.

Unlike most problems, the challenge to rescue Earth from the global warming problem will involve almost every occupation and every country. It will be the biggest project that human beings have ever tackled together. It will involve biologists, chemists, ecologists, atmospheric physicists, industrialists, agriculturists, government officials, social scientists, economists, elected officials, developing nations, big industrial nations, car drivers, consumers, and YOU.

Only by acting together, with each one of us taking what action we can, will the problem be solved.

The air-conditioning costs of residences (and consequent emission of greenhouse gases) in a city (left) *are many times higher than those in a well-planned sub-urban development* (right), *which has numerous trees to keep it cool.*

Chapter 7

Taking Action

A writer in *Car & Driver* wrote, "Global warming is just one more rewrite of the old Chicken Little fable, I reckon, and it will prove to be just as laughable. . . . Of course, I could be wrong."

If global warming is no "Chicken Little fable," we have a major problem on our hands. Solving the problem seems as if it should be the province of governments. But we can't wait for governments to act. Every one of us helped create the global warming conditions. Every one of us has to take action to correct the situation. Laws will eventually be passed that will limit fossil-fuel use on a large scale, but we as individuals have to make changes now.

Many of the actions will be directed toward using less energy than we have in the past. They're not even very dramatic changes. But they are a matter of changing our habits in simple ways.

Taking Personal Action

The things you can do to help the global warming situation are really pretty simple, and they won't affect your lifestyle much at all.

1. Turn off lights in your home, at school or in business offices when a room is not being used. Even if you think you will return to the room in just a few minutes, turn off the lights in case you are detained.

2. Lighting uses about 20 percent of the electricity brought into your home. It's more efficient to use one big light bulb than three or four smaller ones in lighting an area. Switch to fluorescent-type compact bulbs for lighting rooms where lights are used for long periods. The bulb costs more in the first place, but the 18-watt fluorescent bulb gives off

all the light of a 75-watt incandescent bulb and lasts thirteen times longer. And its use will keep almost 300 pounds (135 kilograms) of carbon out of the atmosphere.

3. Turn down the temperature in your home in winter by at least 2 degrees F. (1 degree C). You probably wouldn't even need an extra sweater to handle that amount. In summer, avoid using your air conditioner. If you must use it, turn the thermostat up 3 degrees F. (1.5 degree C).

4. Check your home for leaks and repair them when possible to prevent heat loss. Working with someone else for safety, move a candle flame around every window and door in your home. If the flame dances, there is outside air coming in. Almost half of the energy used to heat our homes is wasted on heating or cooling air that shouldn't be in the house in the first place. See your local power company about a complete energy audit on your house. It will cost perhaps $15 or $20 but will save much more in energy costs. According to Worldwatch, as much energy is lost through leaky

A thermogram is a special photograph of a building that reveals where heat is leaking. This house gives off heat at its windows and along the ceiling line of the basement, where not enough insulation was used when the house was built.

windows in American buildings as flows through the Alaskan pipeline each year.

5. Recycle as much as you possibly can, and be sure to buy recycled products. Recycling glass, paper, plastics, aluminum, and steel costs a lot less in energy and natural resources than using new minerals and fibers each time. Recycling also keeps trash out of landfills, which produce methane, a greenhouse gas.

6. Stay away from products that use CFCs in their manufacture. For example, spray-foam party streamers and aerosol "bullhorns" are made with CFCs. Don't buy them. If in doubt, look for an "ozone-friendly" label on a can.

7. Make certain that air-conditioner or refrigerator repair persons capture and reuse CFCs instead of releasing them into the atmosphere.

8. Move your refrigerator away from sunlight or a warm outside wall to keep it from working so hard. It also has to work harder when it is empty than when it is full.

9. Buy fire extinguishers without halons for both your kitchen and your car. Halons are fire-suppressing chemicals related to CFCs and just as damaging to the atmosphere.

10. Turn your hot-water heater down 10 degrees F. (5.5 degrees C), and then take shorter showers. Hot-water heaters are the second-biggest energy user in the home. Help yours cut its appetite for fossil fuels by putting an insulation jacket on it from your local hardware store. Use low-flow shower heads and faucet heads. They use about half as much hot water as freely flowing ones and do not affect the cleaning power of water.

11. Buy a push-type lawnmower instead of a gasoline-driven one. It's better exercise and you'll keep as much as 30

pounds (14 kilograms) of carbon dioxide out of the atmosphere. Consider planting wildflower gardens or other natural areas that do not require fertilizer or mowing. Such plants use up more carbon dioxide than grasses do, so you're giving the planet a double helping.

12. Plant trees wherever possible on your own land, especially on the south and west sides of your house. Persuade your school or any groups to which you belong to organize tree-planting on public lands in your community. Trees cool by their presence—cutting back on the air conditioning required by nearby buildings—and take carbon dioxide from the atmosphere.

13. If you are among the 28 million Americans who live in apartment buildings, you can conserve energy on your own as well as help convince the management to take energy-saving measures. Keep your thermostat down, especially when no one is home. Cover your windows with taped plastic. Never leave your air conditioners running when you are not home.

Traveling

1. Cut down on car use. You may not be the driver, but you are a member of the family who frequently needs to be driven. Walk whenever possible. Ride your bike. Plan ahead and arrange to car-pool with friends. Plan to do errands in one trip, so that your car is used fewer times each week.

2. Automotive experts say that car engines run most efficiently at 55 mph (89 kph). Anything over or under that speed uses more fuel over the same distance. Encourage your state to reinstate the 55-mph (89-kph) speed limit—it cuts down on traffic fatalities, too.

These students are participating in a tree-planting day for their community. Millions of trees need to be planted every year to help combat global warming.

3. If your family uses a light truck, minivan, or van instead of a car, switch to a car when it's time to replace your vehicle—and make sure that it gets at least 35 miles per gallon (14.8 kilometers per liter). Light trucks are not required to have the same fuel efficiency as automobiles, and they are, in fact, about one-third less efficient. If you can, do without an air conditioner in your new car. You'll save on CFCs and get better mileage.

4. If you have an air-conditioning unit in your car, keep it in good condition. Leaks are among the top sources of CFCs going into the upper atmosphere. If it needs to be repaired, take it to a service station that recycles CFCs. Car-supply firms sell cans of CFCs just so that people can refill their air conditioners themselves. Very few people manage to keep all the CFCs contained when they do this. Try to persuade your local auto-parts dealer not to carry these cans. Ask your government representatives to pass a law banning such cans.

5. Make sure the car itself is always in good condition, with the engine tuned for efficient burning of gasoline.

6. Persuade your parents to become involved in ride-sharing programs. Sixteen states fund such programs, help-

ing people find rides to share and promoting them. In addition, nine states have major cities where only those cars with more than one person in them are allowed to drive on special, faster lanes.

7. Better yet, use mass transit whenever possible. A bus carrying 30 people emits a lot less CO_2 per person than 15 cars carrying 2 people each. If you know you're going to need a ride somewhere, arrange to car-pool or plan your schedule so that you can take buses or trains.

Shop Wisely

1. Buy products made from recycled materials and from materials that can be recycled.

2. Choose natural products such as wood, wool, and cotton over plastics or synthetic fabrics.

3. Choose cushions, pillows, and mattresses not made with foam. They are generally made with CFCs, whereas the fluff-filled ones are not. Even better, though more expensive, return to feather-filled cushions.

4. Buy all items for long use and durability rather than for momentary fads and styles. Otherwise, they end up being thrown away too soon.

5. Look for the most energy-efficient appliances. The products that are energy-efficient will be made and distributed only if the public demands them. You are part of that public and you need to make your wishes known.

6. Sometimes the most obvious purchase is not the most helpful for the environment. For example, an electric shaver uses less energy in a year than it takes to heat hot water for shaving with a regular razor in a week. So the power-using equipment saves more energy.

Express Your Opinion

Encourage your parents and their friends to vote for representatives who have a record of real action in doing something about global warming.

Find out if there are controversies going on in your area about power plants, landfills, or other public utilities that might affect global warming.

Let your public officials, both elected and appointed, know exactly what you think. Many officials are unwilling to take the steps necessary to start large-scale changes in energy use because such changes will temporarily cut business profits. But if enough constituents express their concern, the officials may take notice and begin to act.

Writing Letters. In writing a letter in which you express your opinion on controversial issues, follow these seven tips:

1. Make your letter one page or less. Cover only one subject in each letter.

2. Introduce yourself and tell why you, personally, are for or against the issue.

3. Be clear and to the point.

4. Be specific on whether you want the person to vote "yes" or "no."

5. Write as an individual. The environmental group you belong to will have already let the legislator know its stand on the issue.

6. When you get a response, write a follow-up letter to re-emphasize your position and give your reaction to your legislator's comments.

7. Write again to thank your legislators if they vote the way you asked them to.

On issues concerning state legislation or to express your opinion about actions taken by your state environmental or natural resources agency, you can write to:

Your local state or provincial legislator. Check at your local library to discover his or her name.

The governor of your state or premier of your province. Write in care of your state or provincial capital.

The director of your department of natural resources or similar environmental agency. Check your local library for the specific person and the address.

On issues concerning federal legislation or to express your opinion about actions taken by the federal government, you can write to:

Your two state senators. Check at your local library to discover their names.

The Honorable _____
U.S. Senate
Washington, D.C. 20510

Your local congressman. Check at your local library to discover his or her name.

The Honorable _____
U.S. House of Representatives
Washington, D.C. 20515

Your local provincial or federal Member of Parliament. Check at your local library to discover his or her name.

The Honorable _____
House of Commons
Ottawa, Ontario K1A 046

The President of the United States. He has the power to veto, or turn down, bills approved by the Senate and the

House of Representatives as well as to introduce bills of his own. He also has final control over what the U.S. Environmental Protection Agency and other agencies do.

President _____
The White House
1600 Pennsylvania Avenue, NW
Washington, D.C. 20501

The Prime Minister of Canada.

The Honorable ———————
House of Commons
Ottawa, Ontario K1A 046

Encourage action at both state or provincial and national levels. The action need not be just toward making laws. It might concern the creation of standards for fossil fuels, such as higher vehicle fuel efficiency, improved lighting efficiency, or industrial efficiency. Or it might concern official means of encouraging the changeover to low-emission fuels, the development of renewable energy sources, the improvement of mass transit, or the thoughtful use of nationally owned forestlands.

Global warming cannot be solved by individual cities, provinces, or states passing laws. It can't even be fixed by the federal government passing laws that we must all obey. The one thing scientists have learned in recent years is that the whole planet is affected by what happens in small localities. This does not mean that the problem is too big to solve. You can start by making changes in your own life that will help the planet. Get your friends to make them, too—and their friends, and their friends. And soon our planet will have a future that our grandchildren will treasure.

Join Organizations. Join environmental organizations concerned with the atmosphere. Find out if they have local chapters that you can belong to. Become active in their concerns. Such groups are listened to on an international basis. By joining, you are saying that you support their work on behalf of the environment. Contact the following:

Alliance to Save Energy, 1725 K St., NW, Washington, D.C. 20006

American Forestry Assn., 1516 P St., NW, Washington, D.C. 20036

Canadian Wildlife Federation, 1673 Carling Ave., Ottawa, Ontario, Canada K2A 3Z1

Environmental Defense Fund, 1616 P St., NW, Washington, D.C. 20036

Greenpeace USA, 1436 U St., NW, Washington, D.C. 20009

National Audubon Society, 801 Pennsylvania Ave., SE, Washington, D.C. 20003

National Wildlife Federation, 1400 16th St., NW, Washington, D.C. 20036

World Wildlife Fund, 1250 24th St., NW, Washington, D.C. 20037, or 60 St. Clair Ave., E., Suite 201, Toronto, Ontario, Canada M4T IN5

We don't know for sure whether "the sky will fall" or not. There are many people who are content to assume that global warming is just a scare tactic. However, an interviewer for *Smithsonian* magazine asked Hans Oeschger, the scientist who developed the ice-core technique of studying ancient air, whether he should be worried about what the mathematical models predict about global warming.

Oeschger replied, "You should be very worried. I don't see any reason why these models shouldn't be right. The chances that we are wrong are smaller and smaller. It is also possible that it is *worse* than the models say."

GLOSSARY

anaerobic – without oxygen. Anaerobic bacteria digest organic material in cows' stomachs or in landfills and give off methane as a by-product.

average global temperature – the average of temperatures from all around the world at a certain point in time; also called *global mean temperature*.

biodiversity – the plentiful supply of different plants and animals on Earth. Global warming is likely to harm Earth's biodiversity.

biomass – wood and other vegetation which is treated to make clean-burning fuel.

C, see **Celsius.**

carbon dioxide (CO_2) – a common gas, taken in by plants and exhaled by animals. The main greenhouse gas, its concentration in the atmosphere has increased from the burning of fossil fuels in power plants and automobiles.

Celsius (C) – a temperature scale based on water freezing at 0 degrees and boiling at 100 degrees, also called *centigrade scale*. 1 degree C = 1.8 degrees Fahrenheit.

CFCs, see **chlorofluorocarbons.**

chlorine (Cl) – a chemical element found, with fluorine, in chlorofluorocarbons. When chlorine reaches the ozone layer in the stratosphere, it splits off and reacts with one of the oxygen atoms in ozone, destroying the ozone. This happens repeatedly, and it is estimated that each chlorine molecule can destroy as many as 100,000 ozone molecules.

chlorofluorocarbons (CFCs) – complex chemical combinations containing the elements carbon, chlorine, and fluorine; often known by their tradename, Freons. They are used to propel other chemicals out of aerosol spray cans, in the manufacture of polystyrene foam, and as cooling agents in refrigerators and air conditioners. They help trap heat in the troposphere and damage the ozone layer in the stratosphere.

deforestation – cutting down or burning the trees and other plant life of a forest. This process eliminates trees needed to protect against global warming and increases global warming by releasing carbon dioxide, methane, and other greenhouse gases into the atmosphere.

ecosystem – the total natural world of a specific group of plants and animals.

emissions – gases or particles released during a chemical process such as burning of a fossil fuel or other chemical.

Environmental Protection Agency (EPA), see **United States Environmental Protection Agency.**

F., see **Fahrenheit.**

Fahrenheit (F.) – a temperature scale based on water freezing at 32 degrees and boiling at 212 degrees. 1 degree F. = 0.56 degree Celsius.

fossil fuels – coal, oil, and natural gas, all of which were formed over millions of years by the compression of ancient plants and animals.

Freons, see **chlorofluorocarbons.**

gasohol – a mixture of regular gasoline and ethanol, an alcohol derived from corn or grain.

geothermal – having to do with heat stored within the Earth. Geothermal heat can be used as an energy source to turn turbines.

glaciation – the buildup of large plains of ice called glaciers, during periods of time when summer is too short to melt the winter's accumulation of snow.

global mean temperature, see **average global temperature.**

greenhouse effect – the trapping of the sun's heat within the atmosphere by certain gases, causing Earth's temperature to be warmer than it would otherwise be.

greenhouse gas – any of the gases that contribute to the greenhouse effect by trapping heat within the atmosphere, including carbon dioxide, methane, nitrous oxide, ozone, and CFCs. The molecules of all greenhouse gases consist of three or more atoms.

halons – chemical substances related to CFCs that are commonly used in fire extinguishers. Halons contain a bromine atom that is destructive in the same way as the chlorine atom of CFCs.

hydroelectric – having to do with the generation of electric power from the energy of falling water at the site of dams and waterfalls.

infrared rays - low-frequency, long-wavelength radiation, beyond the red in the visible portion of the spectrum; heat energy.

latitude – distance north or south of the equator, expressed in degrees of a circle.

methane (CH_4) – the major component of natural gas, and a normal trace gas within the atmosphere. An important greenhouse gas, methane is released by the burning of wood and coal and is a product of anaerobic decomposition.

nitrous oxide (N_2O) – a greenhouse gas derived from burning wood and the use of chemical fertilizers on crops.

Organization of Petroleum Exporting Countries (OPEC) – a group of nations that own and export oil. They joined together in order to keep prices and supplies regulated.

ozone (O_3) – a molecule of three oxygen atoms, formed by the action of sunlight on oxygen. Ozone in the lower atmosphere can be harmful to living things, but it is necessary in the upper atmosphere to prevent dangerous ultraviolet rays in sunlight from reaching the Earth.

ozone layer – the region of the atmosphere approximately 22 miles (35 kilometers) above the Earth where ozone tends to accumulate.

photosynthesis – the process by which plants take in carbon dioxide and water, and, in the presence of sunlight, turn them into sugar, which is used by the planet for energy. Oxygen is given off.

photovoltaic – capable of producing electricity by the action of light on special materials. Photovoltaic cells, also called solar cells, and panels are useful in many products as a clean source of energy.

phytoplankton – microscopic plant life that is the base of the ocean food chain.

polar ice cap – a huge accumulation of ice at the North or South Pole, especially the glacial covering of the Antarctic continent.

smog – hazy air pollution made up of various gases, chemicals, and dust.

solar thermal energy – energy derived from capturing the heat of sunlight. It can be used directly to heat buildings or indirectly to make steam to turn the turbines that generate electricity.

stratosphere – the upper level of the Earth's atmosphere, above the region where weather is formed. Within the stratosphere is the ozone layer.

sulfur dioxide – a pollutant caused by burning. In the atmosphere, it increases cloud cover and is blamed for acid rain.

temperate – moderate, mild; located in the middle latitudes. In the north the Temperate Zone is the region between the Tropic of Cancer and the Arctic Circle; in the south, between the Tropic of Capricorn and the Antarctic Circle.

trace gases – gases such as water vapor, carbon dioxide, methane, and ozone, which together make up the 1 percent of air that is not oxygen or nitrogen.

tropical – located in or typical of the tropics, the region between the parallels of latitude 23 1/2 degrees north and south of the equator, the region sometimes called the Torrid Zone.

troposphere – the lowest level of Earth's atmosphere, where temperatures change and the planet's weather occurs.

ultraviolet rays – radiated energy with short wavelengths, beyond the violet in the visible portion of the spectrum.

United States Environmental Protection Agency (EPA) – a federal government agency whose job is to regulate factors of the environment and those that may be affecting it.

UV-B – abbreviation for the form of ultraviolet rays that is harmful to living things. The ozone layer keeps it from reaching Earth's surface.

wetlands – low-lying marshes and lagoons that flood part or all of the year. They may be salt water or fresh water. Many plants and animals depend on wetlands for food and breeding grounds.

INDEX

Bold number = Illustration

126

PHOTO SOURCES

Agricultural Research Service/United States Department of Agriculture: 66
American Cancer Society: 84
Courtesy of American Petroleum Institute: 29, 93, 100
Ask Corporation: 82
William H. Brune, Penn State: 80
Don Cabrera/Bureau of Land Management: 13
Chicago Transit Authority: 95
Ralph Clark: 10
Coastal Management Division, Louisiana Department of Natural Resources: 60, 62
Coastal Restoration Division, Louisiana Department of Natural Resources: 61 (left)
Courtesy of the Danish Tourist Board: 34
S.C. Delaney/EPA: 14, 75
Florida Game and Fresh Water Fish Commission: 9
Tiana Glenn/Boise Interagency Fire Center: 2, 6
Elizabeth B. Graf: 25
Peggy Hallward, Probe International: 63
Illinois Eye Institute: 86
Industry, Science and Technology, Canada, Photo/Near Strathmore, Alberta: 67
Dr. Stephen P. Leatherman/Laboratory for Coastal Research, University of Maryland at College Park: 52, 55, 69 (both)
The Louisiana Land & Exploration Co.: 51 (both), 61 (right)
James MacArthur, Chief of Bureau of Shade Tree Management/Department of Environmental Manage ment: 109 (both)
National Aeronautics and Space Administration: 31 (top), 38, 40, 47, 57, 58, 59, 77, 78 (top, bottom left), 79 (top left, top right)
National Center for Atmospheric Research/National Science Foundation: 44, 45
National Oceanic and Atmospheric Administration: 41
NOAA's Marine Debris Information Office: 50
National Park Service photo by Richard Frear: 19
Netherlands Board of Tourism: 110
Northeast Sustainable Energy Association: 94 (right)
Osage, Iowa, Municipal Utilities: 112
Photocomm, Grass Valley, California: 102 (top right, middle)
Salt River Project: 96
Sandia National Laboratories: 90
Soil Conservation Service, United States Department of Agriculture: 23, 28
Solarex: 102 (bottom right, bottom left)
Solarex and Pompes Guinard: 102 (top left)
Todd Sowers/University of Rhode Island: 43
State Historical Society of Wisconsin: 37
Allen Stenstrup/Havenwoods Environmental Center: 115
Darin Toohey/Harvard University: 70, 78 (bottom right), 79 (bottom)
U.S. Windpower, Inc., Livermore, California: 101
United Nations Photo 164623/John Isaac: 68 (right)
United States Department of Agriculture: 21 (right), 49
United States Department of Agriculture Forest Service/ Pacific Northwest Region: 32, 65, 107
United States Department of Energy: 27, 94 (left), 99, 105
Pieter Wiebe, Woods Hole Oceanographic Institution: 87
Terri Willis: 92
World Bank Photo Library: 21 (left), 31 (bottom), 68 (left)

ABOUT THE AUTHORS

Jean F. Blashfield and Wallace B. Black are dedicated environmentalists, writers, and publishers who are responsible for this book and the *SAVING PLANET EARTH* series. Working together, with other environmentalists, educators, and Childrens Press, they have developed 13 other books in the *SAVING PLANET EARTH* series.

This creative team was responsible for the creation of *THE YOUNG PEOPLE'S SCIENCE ENCYCLOPEDIA* and *ABOVE AND BEYOND, THE ENCYCLOPEDIA OF AVIATION AND SPACE SCIENCES*. In addition, Jean Blashfield was the editor-in-chief of *THE YOUNG STU-DENTS ENCYCLOPEDIA* and is author of more than 20 other books. Wallace Black, a former pilot in the United States Air Force, is the author of a series of books on World War II.